Take Hold
of
Your Life

Take Hold of Your Life

B.W. Woods

BAKER BOOK HOUSE
Grand Rapids, Michigan

To my son **Mark**, the theologian,
and
to my daughter **Debra**, the lawyer,
who light up my life.

Acknowledgments

This book has grown out of twenty-three years of ministry. I shall forever be indebted to those individuals who have touched my life, called me "Pastor," shared with me their inner burdens, and most of all, inspired me with their unquenchable joy. Of these happy people, most were of very modest means; some lived in poverty. But they were happy, in spite of trials and heartbreaks, because they were in control of their lives. Their quiet lives were grounded in a firm faith which had its roots in the Holy Scriptures. In my attempts to minister to them, I found them ministering to me. This is at best a feeble effort to pay tribute to those good people.

A special note of appreciation is due my secretary, Mrs. Ann Wheeler, who went far beyond her required duties during the typing and retyping of this manuscript.

Contents

> He that hath no rule over his own
> spirit is like a city that is broken
> down, and without walls.
> (Prov. 25:28)

1
Take Control
of Your Life

■Picture for a moment a heavily loaded runaway freight train coming into a busy station with no one at the controls. Or suppose while driving on the highway you meet an eighteen-wheeler coming full speed down a long hill without any driver in the cab. Each of these possibilities vividly portrays the danger of a life out of control. Much of the human wreckage we see strewn all about us is the result of lives going full speed with no one at the controls.

The reason for long countdowns prior to spacecraft liftoffs is to get everything under control. The guidance system with all its scientific checks and counterbalances must be in order. If a spacecraft is to reach its destiny, a great deal of care must be given to the guidance system. This is the case with humans, too, yet many people

Spirit - soul, frame of mind

choose to live at full speed without any regard for traffic signals or road maps.

The writer of Proverbs issued a solemn warning on this point: "He that hath no rule over his own spirit is like a city that is broken down, and without walls" (Prov. 25:28). In ancient times a city could not exist long without walls and fortifications. Such a city would be sacked and destroyed, would become the pawn of some despot. Any person who is unable to control his own spirit is in the same precarious situation. *cruel ruler*

If you don't care what happens to yourself or what you become, who do you suppose will care? Who really should care, if you don't? Unless you are in control of your life, no one is, for only you are with yourself every moment of every day in every place.

THE PRINCIPLE OF SELF-CONTROL

basic truth
moral standards

The free-wheeling life sooner or later self-destructs. You are surrounded by the powers of darkness, by the temptations of Satan, by your own inner weaknesses. Unless you determine to "rule your own spirit," you will find yourself in the grip of the powers of darkness. The quality and future of your life is at stake; eternity is at stake. Self-control will determine whether you will look back on life rejoicing or cursing the day of your birth.

* It was said of Moses, the man who defied Pharaoh, that he was meek "above all the men which were upon the face of the earth" (Num. 12:3). Meekness is life under control. Christ said, "Blessed are the meek: for they shall inherit the earth" (Matt. 5:5). Jesus was saying that all of

challenged

life awaits the person who is able to control and guide the drives that lie within him.

The apostle Paul was the greatest missionary ever. On one occasion he shared his secret for being able to accomplish so much: "I keep under my body, and bring it into subjection: lest that by any means, when I have preached to others, I myself should be a castaway" (I Cor. 9:27). He realized that he could ruin his future, his usefulness in the kingdom of God, if he failed to rule his own spirit well. If he wanted to do the best things in life, there were some lesser things he could not afford to become involved in.

If we are to walk the narrow way that leads to life, we must not go down any forks in the road. Negatives are small reflectors along the edge of that highway in dangerous places. Lesslie Newbigin has reminded us that negatives are "like the fence which protects the traveler from falling over the edge into the ravine below."[1] The mark of maturity is not to see how near one can get to the edge without going over. A child asks, "How much can I get away with?" But an adult asks, "What is worth having? What journey is worth making? What goal is worth striving for?"

Paul used the world of athletics to speak of the necessary discipline needed for achieving his own personal goals. He noted that everyone in a race should run in an effort to win, and that everyone who wants to master any sport must be serious about it, must pay the price of training. In this light, he said, "I keep under my body, and bring it into subjection" (I Cor. 9:27).

Anyone who takes Jesus Christ seriously, who tries to live the godly life, must recognize that such a task is not easy. Ernest Campbell emphasized this as he told about hearing a religious disk jockey one Sunday morning close his program with a cheery benediction: "Remember, things go better with God." The intentions of the disk jockey were probably the very best, but the meaning of this phrase could be harmful to the Christian life.

Of course he was using a take-off on the Coke slogan, "things go better with Coke." According to commercials that use the slogan, whatever you happen to be doing or eating, Coke is a welcome accompaniment that adds enjoyment. It is a condiment, an addition to add flavor just as mustard, salt, and spices do. If we take the disk jockey's words literally, he was telling us that God is an extra, an option, that can add some flavor to what you are doing.

Imagine the disk jockey shouting his word of encouragement to Moses in the wilderness when the Israelites were murmuring against him and plotting to return to Egypt. Imagine giving such an encouragement to Job sitting atop his ash heap, scraping the boils that covered his body and mourning the loss of his children. How does this admonition fit the apostle Paul as he suffered constantly from his "thorn in the flesh"? Imagine how the disk jockey's words would have sounded to Simon Peter who, according to tradition, was crucified head down because of his faith.

The truth is, those who dare to follow Christ may find that many things do not always go better. To follow Christ is sometimes to travel upstream or to go against the tide. If life with Christ were the easy life, everyone would follow him. However, the good life is a difficult, yet rewarding life. Only those who are willing to rule their own spirit, to exercise self-control, can live it.

use
THE APPLICATION OF SELF-CONTROL

The great throngs of society follow the ancient philosophy of the Corinthians: "Meats for the belly, and the belly for meats" (I Cor. 6:13). By this, the Corinthians meant that since one has certain human appetites, they were meant to be fulfilled. Therefore one does whatever feels good and assumes that it is the right way to live. Their philosophy of life was "do what you want," but the Christian philosophy of life is "do what you ought." There is a world of difference, and this difference needs to be noted in several important areas.

Personality development. The person you become is directly related to whether or not you choose to exercise self-control over your life. Paul countered the philosophy of the Corinthians with: "All things are lawful unto me, but all things are not expedient: all things are lawful for me, but I will not be brought under the power of any" (I Cor. 6:12). The apostle refused to become a slave to anything, including bad habits and evil temptations. He refused to be a part of anything that was not "expedient" (the word *expedient* refers to something that is able to carry its own weight and make a contribution) or was enslaving.   1. advantageous
2. convenient

Your personality develops only on the same ratio with which you grow in maturity. Maturity is a willingness to postpone fulfillment of present desires, and self-control governs the growth of maturity. One either learns to rule his own spirit, to control himself, to postpone the fulfillment of present desires, or he takes into his life everything that presents itself. The opposite of self-control is seen when children throw tantrums, for tantrums are designed to get what one wants. The child says, "I want what I want now, or I will throw a tantrum." Tragically, the world is filled with adults who still operate by the same principle.

You will never discover the real you, never grow to be your unique self, until you are willing to exercise self-control. You have to be willing to build enough fences around the inner core of your soul to keep the world from trampling across. You either separate yourself enough to become an individual, or you remain a blur in the crowd. ✶ Our society is marked by an attitude of unwillingness to wait for fulfillment and unwillingness to pay the price which proper fulfillment requires. For instance, most stealing takes place because people are not willing to earn the goods they want, or they are not willing to wait until they can afford them. Most young people who run away from home do so because they are not willing to wait until they grow up to go out on their own. They are not willing to live under the authority of their parents until they have reached an age of maturity. Drugs are taken by different people for different reasons: sometimes by those who can't wait to see if life can be fulfilled without the exhilaration of the drugs, and sometimes by those who are not willing to pay the price of facing the real world. Premarital sex is engaged in by people who refuse to wait for the God-ordained means of sexual fulfillment. The wholesomeness of one's personality development depends on one's willingness to exercise self-control.

Drug usage. Usage of and dependence on drugs is an increasing problem in the lives of millions of people. *Drugs* is a broad term that covers anything from beer to heroin. Some people use drugs because they think they lead to exciting new adventures; these people can't wait to see if God will bring happiness in His own time. On the other hand, some take drugs because they are not willing to face the real world or their real selves. We are developing a society that is dependent in one way or another on drugs. In fact, we may take pills to pep us up, slow us down, keep us awake, and put us to sleep.

➤ Life is meant to be a trust whereby we are willing to allow God to bring into our life the exhilaration and the strength that is needed for our particular situations. The use of drugs is an effort to manufacture a make-believe world that sooner or later will crash. Huxley, in his *Brave New World*, pictures a society where all the rough edges are removed by the use of a drug called "soma." Soma is the name of a drug mentioned in the Vedas of Hinduism and was apparently akin to the mescaline-type drug developed from a mushroom in Byblos around 3000 B.C. Indeed, many of the ancient pagan religions made use of mind-expanding drugs. Peyote was divine to the Aztecs, coca to the Incas, soma to the Hindus, and ambrosia to the Greeks. As Baudelaire put it, man has always searched for shortcuts, for "paradise in a single sweet."[2] Anyone who builds his world around drugs is building a world that someday will crash.

<u>Sexual morality.</u> One of the great problem areas of our society is sexual immorality. The sociologist Pitirim Sorokin wrote in *American Sex Revolution* that "every phase of our culture has become invaded by sex. Our civilization has become so preoccupied with sex that it now oozes from all pores of American life." He goes on to say that man's preoccupation with sex has undermined physical and mental health and has disrupted our finest social institutions.

When German theologian Helmut Thielicke visited the United States a few years ago, he told reporters that the major problem he found in America was that Americans refuse to deal with the presence and role of suffering in life. As an example he referred to a young person who becomes awakened to sex before he or she is mature and able to consider marriage. Because of the teachings of Scripture, such a young person must control sexual drives until they can be fulfilled in marriage. Yet many young people are unwilling to bear the problem, to put off fulfillment until sex may be experienced in the proper way. Supposing there is a pill for every answer, the young person takes for granted that oral contraceptives give sway to sexual freedom. And society has already decided that when a young person fails to use the pills correctly and pregnancy does occur, that no suffering should be endured—abortion is the answer.[3]

Sex has lost its sacredness and has become a national sport. At the heart of the matter lies the question of whether or not a person decides to respect himself or herself. Self-control postpones sexual fulfillment until it can be done in decency and with the approval of God. A prostitute is held in disrepute, but is it not as bad or worse to give oneself to any and everyone as opportunity arises? To do this is to make one's life like a vacant lot through which anyone can pass. This makes the heart little more than a hardened path strewn with litter. I remember hearing a young person several years ago share the heartbreak that came to her in the breaking of God's moral laws. She said that the worst part was not the fear of pregnancy, but the loss of self-respect.

In addition to self-respect, which comes only by keeping God's law, there is another important aspect: respect for others. A person engaged in sexual immorality sees other people as instruments of self-gratification. He or she refuses to look upon them as individuals with hopes and dreams, with future destinies, with personalities that can be ruined and shattered. The old professor in Pilgrim's

Progress sat in an iron cage, a man of despair. When asked how he had come to that sad condition he explained: "I left off to watch and be sober; I laid the reins upon the neck of my lust; I sinned against the light of the word and the goodness of God; I have grieved the Spirit, and He is gone; I tempted the devil, and he has come to me; I have provoked God to anger, and He has left me; I have so hardened my heart, that I cannot repent."

In addition to giving importance to respecting yourself, and respecting others, there is a third vital element that comes to play at the point of sexual morality—reverence for God. A person's morality is a direct reflection of his or her relationship to God. Pagans have always indulged in sexual looseness, but one of the main characteristics of a person who follows Christ is sexual purity. The early Christians stood in direct contrast to the world of paganism that surrounded them. When the early Christians met in council at Jerusalem to determine what was necessary for salvation, their consensus was that a man can be saved through a faith commitment to Jesus Christ. Yet they ordered that all Christians be reminded that to follow Christ meant forsaking any adulterous activities. Scripture says: "This is the will of God, even your sanctification, that you should abstain from fornication" (I Thess. 4:3). Again Scripture affirms: "But whoso committeth adultery with a woman lacketh understanding: he that doeth it destroyeth his own soul" (Prov. 6: 32). Nothing shatters life any more than living in immorality.

THE STRENGTH FOR SELF-CONTROL

Our original text (Prov. 25:28) warned against a man having no rule over his own spirit, because he would be "like a city that is broken down, and without walls." We can have more than human strength to rule our spirit with, for our heavenly Father will give us as much strength as we allow Him to. The Christian life is the self-controlled life, guided and empowered by the risen, living Christ. We can say with the apostle Paul, "I can do all things *through* [*Christ*] who strengthens me" (Phil. 4:13, NASB, italics mine). The apostle also said in the same letter: "Being confident of this very thing, that he which hath begun a good work in you will perform it until the day of Jesus Christ" (Phil. 1:6).

✷ When we make our commitment to Christ we should be able to say with the apostle, "I am crucified with Christ: nevertheless I live; yet not I, but Christ liveth in me: and the life which I now live in the flesh I live by the faith of the Son of God, who loved me, and gave himself for me" (Gal. 2:20). We must step out of the wings, go to center stage, and announce to Satan and all the forces of evil that in the name of Jesus Christ, and in the power of His presence, we are taking control of our lives.

✷ We can be "reactors" and respond to whatever pressures are being applied to us. We can blame circumstances, cruel fate, or other people for our problems, but there is a better option: we can accept responsibility for our actions. We can accept the difficulties and discouragements that are ours as a challenge God has uniquely prepared us to overcome. It will be worth whatever price is demanded.

Once we are willing to take control, make our own choices, do what we feel is important instead of what seems easiest, we will respect ourselves in a way never known before. We may lose some people we thought were friends (but we will lose no real friends). We may drop some meaningless activities and some destructive habits.

In fact, we may develop whole new lifestyles. We will rearrange our schedules in light of our own priorities instead of by peer pressure. We will be in a position to stop wondering why we have been dealt our particular circumstances, and start centering in on what Christ would have us do with them.

The most meaningful experiences of life are usually those that are difficult and shattering. In the darkness we often see more fully who we are and what we ought to be. As a rule, we will minister to others out of our weaknesses, not out of our strengths. Others can identify with our weaknesses. If we dare to assume control of our lives, accept the responsibility for them, and face our weaknesses, we shall discover the power of a greater presence. Our heavenly Father does not empower us to deal with all the problems of the world, but He does give us special grace to deal with those that are peculiarly ours. Our own struggles will in turn inspire others to take hope and take control.

Nels Ferre, the famous theologian who died a few years ago, grew up in Norway. At age thirteen, he was invited to come to the United States to live with an aunt and uncle who could give him an education which his poverty-stricken parents could never do. Therefore his parents accepted the offer and made preparations to send Nels to the United States. It was a wrenching experience for a boy of thirteen to leave his native land and his parents, knowing that he might never see them again.

Although Nels was very close to his mother, she said very little to him during the preparation for his journey. He kept waiting for her to give him some word of encouragement, some word to sustain him in the days that lay ahead. All through supper the night before he was to leave, he kept yearning for some word from her, but there was nothing but silence. He went to bed that night and cried himself to sleep. The next morning during breakfast, and during the ride on the cart to the village, there was still no word from her. It was not until he was on the train, and the train was beginning to move, that his mother started to run alongside. She called up to him through his open window these brief words: "Nels, remember Jesus. Remember Jesus."

Times and events take us places we have never gone before, throw us into the midst of strangers, smother us with feelings of loneliness, yet in the midst of all of it, we do well to heed the simple words of Nels Ferre's mother: "Remember Jesus. Remember Jesus." If we do, we will have a life under control.

This book is an aid to help you take control of your own life. You don't have to live passively. You can be in control. You must fill your life with those characteristics and elements that produce wholeness and usefulness, regardless of outward circumstances. It can be done, and I dare you to try it!

NOTES

1. Lesslie Newbigin, *Honest Religion for Secular Man* (Philadelphia: The Westminster Press, 1966), p. 143.

2. Os Guinness, *The Dust of Death* (Downers Grove, IL: Inter-Varsity Press, 1973), pp. 233–34.

3. Helmut Thielicke, *Between Heaven and Earth* (Westport, CT: Greenwood Press Publishers, 1965), pp. 184–89.

It was meet that we should
make merry, and be glad. . . .
(Luke 15:32)

2

Examine Your Concepts of Happiness and Unhappiness

■If someone asked you for a formula for happiness, what would you suggest? Such a question would force you to come to grips with your own concepts of happiness and unhappiness.

A careful study of Scripture indicates that many of us have faulty concepts. We discover that to set out in direct pursuit of happiness is to fail. Happiness comes as a by-product of a certain kind of life built around vital ingredients.

First, let's take a look at the misconceptions of what happiness is.

STORYBOOK HAPPINESS

Selfish. The twentieth-century concept of happiness is usually marked by selfishness. To the average person, happiness means a life free from worry and sadness, marked by good health, a nice home, a good marriage relationship, and socially accepted, well-married children. Someone has noted that "the only difference between a man and a boy is that a man's toys cost more."[1] For the immature man, happiness is being surrounded by toys. His basic prayer of such happiness is, "God bless me and my wife, my son John and his wife, us four and no more."

Unrealistic. Storybook happiness is unrealistic in that it supposes we can live in our world and be insulated from its cries of pain and suffering. It ignores the struggle between good and evil, between God and Satan, that goes on beneath the surface of our society, and beneath the surface of our own lives. It is blind to the inner life which alone can produce real happiness. We are beguiled into thinking that man's pursuit of happiness can be equated with man's pursuit of things. Walter Reuther speaks of America becoming a circus civilization devoting itself to "communal happiness hunts."[2]

Short-lived. The wall built around one's selfish kingdom sooner or later crumbles. When this happens, happiness is gone for that person, because he is left alone without God and without hope for eternal life.

The Bible does not promise storybook happiness to Christians. Indeed, if a person has had a true salvation experience, he could not possibly enjoy this kind of isolated happiness in the midst of a world of need. The pursuit of storybook happiness leaves many people disillusioned and cynical about life, because they are pursuing something that God never intended and never promised.

GENUINE HAPPINESS

Someone has declared that the gnawing fear of Puritanism was that someone, somewhere, might be happy. This has too often characterized the world's concept of Christianity. Yet it is God's will that His people have genuine happiness.

Interestingly, the Bible has no word that really corresponds to our English word *happiness*. When English translations contain the word *happiness* it is a translation of the Greek word *makarios*. In the Old Testament, *makarios* marks the happiness of one who is near God and trusts, loves, and fears Him. It is always identified with those of pure character. The word has behind it the awareness that sin is the fountainhead of all misery. The man in the Scriptures who is happy realizes that happiness is based on faith and love, not on knowledge.

In the Beatitudes introducing the Sermon on the Mount, *makarios* is translated as "blessed." Thus genuine happiness is a kind of inward glow and sense of well-being based on one's relationship to God. It is a joy that grows out of an awareness that one's sins have been forgiven and one's destiny assured (Rom. 4:7).

The Beatitudes list some positive steps for producing a happy life. The meek man—one who channels and directs his strength to control himself and maintain his identity—has the kingdom of heaven (participation in all the blessings of the new covenant and in the blessings of glory above). The man who cares for others will be comforted in that his Father also cares for him. The man who recognizes his spiritual need will have his needs met. The merciful man will receive mercy. The man who has made the decisions that allow him to be pure in heart will see God. The peacemaker will be called a child of God. The man who takes his stand even when it means hardship or persecution will receive a reward in heaven. The Beatitudes conclude by saying that the happy life is one that becomes salt in the midst of corruption and light in the midst of darkness (Matt. 5:1–16).

Following are some characteristics of genuine happiness.

Unselfish. Someone has said, "Happy is the man who finds a task to do, for his hands are not idle; happy is the man who finds another to help, for his heart is not idle; happy is the man who finds something creative to do, for then his mind is not idle. Happiness is keeping the hands, the heart, and the mind in motion—creative and purposeful motion."[3]

Genuine happiness comes from caring for others and serving them and God. Centuries ago, Pericles said; "Happiness is freedom and freedom is courage." As we give ourselves we find freedom; and as we lose ourselves we find life.

In Jesus' vivid picture of the judgment, He said that His children will be recognized as those who met the needs of the world about them, who fed the hungry and gave water to the thirsty, who visited the sick, clothed the naked, and ministered to those in prison. In contrast, the miserable ones will be those who built a fence around themselves and isolated themselves from the pain of the world (Matt. 25).

Realistic. A biblically happy man sees the struggle and

evil in the world, but sees the good and opportunity as well. Edwin Markham has a poem entitled "Shoes of Happiness" in which an Oriental sultan, ill and depressed, was advised to find a happy man and wear his shoes. After much searching, the sultan found a happy man, but the problem was, the man had no shoes.

The apostle Paul admonished Christians to "*rejoice in the Lord alway*" (Phil. 4:4, italics mine). *Joy* is a better word to describe Christian happiness. The same chapter in which Paul admonished the Philippians to rejoice, depicts the quarreling between two women, Euodias and Syntyche. The chapter speaks of anxieties, of being in need, and of being abased. Yet it says we are to keep our eyes on the good about us: "Finally, brethren, whatsoever things are true, whatsoever things are honest, whatsoever things are just, whatsoever things are pure, whatsoever things are lovely, whatsoever things are of good report; if there be any virtue, and if there be any praise, think on these things" (Phil. 4:8). One can rejoice in the midst of all kinds of experiences because of the assurance that "my God shall supply all your need according to his riches and glory by Christ Jesus" (Phil. 4:19).

Eternal. Deep and abiding joy, genuine happiness, grows out of one's relationship to Jesus Christ. To be "in Christ" is to be in an existence larger than our threescore years and ten. The Christian can honestly rejoice in the most trying circumstances, even at the funeral of a Christian loved one, because of the promise of a resurrection. The Christian can rejoice even if his x-rays reveal a malignancy, because he knows about an eternity beyond these brief years. He can live in a world marked by starvation and disease, catastrophe and evil, yet not become cynical, because he also sees the heavenly Father at work and knows there will be a new heaven and a new earth.

THE SIN OF UNHAPPINESS

The sin of unhappiness is portrayed by the elder brother in a well-known parable told by our Lord. The story bears repeating: The wayward son, "the prodigal," has returned from the far country where he has run through his share of the family fortune in one fast fling. Now he has come home repentant, humiliated, and penniless. The father has welcomed the wayward son with open arms, killed the fatted calf, and thus is staging the biggest social event the community has ever seen.

The elder brother stands in the shadows, looking in, but refusing to enter. Far too many of us stand in the curse of his lineage. Take a close look at the elder brother. This young man would have given you quite an earful over a cup of coffee. His sad story would have been one extravaganza of wallowing in self-pity. He would have told you about the years of faithful service he had rendered the father and how it had gone without any tangible evidence of appreciation. He would have told you about the injustice of life that seems to reward the sinful and ignore the righteous.

A multitude of sins immediately comes to mind when we consider the wayward son, but the elder's sin is, of all things, unhappiness. This is a strange thought, because we do not usually think of unhappiness as a sin. We usually see the "unhappy" in terms of those who have been mistreated, have not received a fair shake, or have been the innocent victims of circumstances.

We discover that neither son really wanted to stay in the father's house. The wayward son left home, and the elder son stayed there, but grumbled within himself about it. He was a great deal like "old Joe" who joined the Salvation Army after having lived as a skid row bum. He immediately gained the task of beating the drum on the street corner with the rest of the band. Some of old Joe's cronies heard about his conversion and remarked among themselves that there didn't seem to be anything sacred anymore. Then with some sense of obligation they hunted Joe up and found him on the street corner beating the drum with the rest of the band.

During the conversation which ensued, Joe told them of his new life—how he had come to a moment of faith, how he no longer was a slave to alcohol—and he concluded by saying, "Now I've got religion, and night after night I stand here beating this stupid drum!"

This was the feeling of the elder brother. All his life he had done what was "right" and had found absolutely no meaning or joy in it. His unhappiness was indeed a sin. Most of us can understand his feelings, for we, too, have tried to do right and have found our efforts to be meaningless.

ATTITUDES PRODUCING THE SIN OF UNHAPPINESS

Self-pity. When the father comes out of the house to plead with the elder son to enter into the rejoicing, the response of the son is, "You never planned a party like this for me!" The elder is surrounded by his own self-pity. Most depression through which people pass is brought on by various kinds of self-pity. The elder felt that he had been mistreated, that there was no justice in the world, that his faithfulness had gone unnoticed and unrewarded. He was much like the psalmist who looked about him, noted that the sinful seemed to get along better than the righteous, that the wicked seemed to have an easier life than the just, and was at the point of utter despair (Ps. 73).

Self-righteousness. The elder brother accuses the prodigal of having spent all of his money on harlots. Whether or not this is so we are not told. The elder sees himself as the good guy in the white hat, and the prodigal as the villain. The fact that the villain has returned in repentance is beside the point.

One characteristic of self-righteousness is that it never offers forgiveness. To forgive a scoundrel is to allow him to become your equal, your brother! The elder would much prefer to see the brother stay afar and get what he deserves. Strange as it is, this attitude is found among some church members who, from within the church, never forgive those who have lived waywardly. The same attitude is found in some who are living outside the church, apart from God, and refuse to enter in because they can't abide the sinners in the church—the hypocrites. In each case, neither is willing to make the other an equal through forgiveness.

Self-centeredness. The law of the day automatically gave to the elder son two-thirds of the father's inheritance. When the prodigal demanded his inheritance ahead of time, the father divided unto each son his inheritance. The prodigal got one-third of the father's wealth; the elder had the remaining two-thirds. The only drawback was that he had to have the father along with the two-thirds as long as the father lived. Thus the elder had—yet didn't have—his inheritance. He worked, he managed well, he kept the rules, he permitted himself no weaknesses, and he put up with the father—and what had it gotten him? The first time the wayward son shows up penniless, the father takes him back in.

Perhaps the attitude of the elder brother is held by those who deplore the federal welfare system. I have noticed that few who complain about the great life people are having on welfare are in any rush to be a part of it, yet all that anyone would have to do to join would be to gather up everything he owns and give it away, then sign up. A man's objection to welfare for others is that he has to pay for that other person's welfare. This is the exact complaint of the elder brother. He has worked hard, and now it is the calf he owns, that he has cared for, that he has fattened, that is providing the food for the celebration of the prodigal's return.

⭐ It is possible for a person to keep all the rules, to be hard-working, thrifty, and decent, yet be utterly unchristian in his attitudes and concerns for others. This sin—self-centeredness—is the sin of the elder brother.

The good that the elder brother does is done grudgingly. He resents his calf being eaten. He resents the attention of his father toward the wayward son. He can't enter into his father's goals in life for the family. He has no thought of the fullness of life and blessings that have come to him by being in his father's house for so many years.

If you are honest enough to see yourself here, there is hope for you. Now let's observe what unhappiness does to one's life.

THE EFFECTS OF THE SIN OF UNHAPPINESS

Loss of perspective. The attitudes that produce the sin of unhappiness bring with them the loss of perspective. Life ceases to have a vision; the world shrinks; blessings go unnoticed.

The elder brother scarcely pays attention to his father as he assures him, "All I have is thine." The elder brother is too busy grudgingly thinking, "All that is left ought to be mine." He has eliminated his father just as much as the prodigal did by leaving home. He has lost sight of the beauty of his father's world.

How often do we, like the elder brother, live oblivious to the mystery of the stars, the song of the birds, the beauty of the sunrise, the silence of the snow. The sin of unhappiness causes the song of life to cease.

The elder brother is like Edgar Allen Poe who, in his poem, "Israfel," speaks of the beautiful melodies Israfel the angel plays on his heavenly lyre and the melodious songs he sings. Poe observes that Israfel has forgotten how bad things are on earth, that Israfel could not have such a song if he lived in a real "world of sweets and sours." Poe then concludes:

> If I could dwell
>   Where Israfel
> Hath dwelt, and he where I,
>   He might not sing so wildly well
> A mortal melody,
>   While a bolder note than this might swell
> From my lyre within the sky.

Stagnation. When a person chooses to live with the

attitudes that produce unhappiness, he ceases to grow. No new experiences come into his life, so the years pass, but nothing really happens to him. And worst of all, he always blames it on someone else, as the elder blamed his father for injustice.

THE ANTIDOTE FOR UNHAPPINESS

Whatever the circumstances of life, if a person lives in unhappiness, it is because he has chosen to do so. The unhappiness of the elder brother is a way of life he has chosen. Hope for him is that he can choose to respond differently. What can break the chains of self-pity, self-righteousness, and self-centeredness? The Bible has the answer: living generously. Unhappiness can be turned around if one determines to be a "giving" person. The secret is the determination to become a blessing instead of a curse. Only the "giving" life escapes uselessness, as indicated by the words of an unknown author:

> There are a lot of men who creep
> Into the world to eat and sleep,
> And know no reason why they're born
> Save only to consume the corn,
> Devour the cattle, bread and fish,
> And leave behind an empty dish;
> And if their tombstones, when they die,
> Were not to flatter or to lie,
> There's nothing better can be said,
> Than that they've eaten up their bread,
> Drunk up their drink, and gone to bed.[4]

In the elder brother's case, giving must take place at these following points.

Give himself totally to the father. The elder has apparently always withheld himself from the father; now he must accept the father's values and perspective. To the father, the welfare of a wayward human being is more important than a fatted calf. The elder must discover that the major goal in life is not to fatten calves, but to live in joy in the father's house. This means the elder must give himself to the calling of being a son in the father's house. Keeping rules are not enough; he must have the spirit of the father as well. At this point we must remind ourselves that the "father" in the parable represents our heavenly Father.

In this kind of giving, the elder can discover afresh the real blessings of sonship. He will realize that he never really missed anything by not going to the far country as his brother did. It is easy to condemn sin, yet feel that we have missed out on a lot of fun by not having had our own fling. The good life is found in daily being with the Father and recognizing all that the Father has He wants to share with us. We read in the first book of the Bible that God's reason for breathing into man the breath of life, was that man might share in His life.

Give himself to his brother in forgiveness. Self-righteousness is destroyed when one forgives and accepts the transgressor as an equal. The elder needs to do some confessing himself. In fact, he may have been part of the reason the wayward son left home. It does not take much imagination to see the elder, even as the boys were growing up, constantly correcting, scolding, and tattling on the younger brother.

Give himself to the party. As long as the elder stood on

the outside, his presence cast a shadow on the father's party. Karl Olson tells how he discovered in himself the spirit of the elder brother, how he realized that all of his life he had somehow felt "unblessed," unaccepted by his own father, and by God. At last in his spiritual pilgrimage he came to the place where he could discover the joy of knowing that he had been accepted by God, that he didn't have to *do* anything—that he had been saved by the grace of God. With that he also came to the realization that he no longer had to try to be someone he couldn't be in order to make it with God. He realized that God loved him as he was—that he could be himself. So he took the elder brother he found within his own heart and buried him in the fields, washed and changed clothes, combed his hair, and entered the father's house where there was music and dancing.[5]

Olson goes on to tell how the church has become for many the "unparty" instead of the joy of the indwelling Spirit of God. Serving in the Father's house must come with a sense of freedom and must be done out of the joy of gratitude—never to earn merit or to save oneself.

The world is filled with elder brothers who never rejoice in the Father's presence, who are selfish even in their religion, who resent giving self or money, who have never determined to make themselves a blessing in the kingdom of God. The prodigal changed his attitude from "give me" to "make me." The elder brother can do the same, and so can we.

The father, when he asks the elder brother to join the party, says, "All I have is thine." But the son is not willing to respond, "And all I have is thine." The happiest people in the Bible are those who chose to live generously. A poor widow with only two small coins gave them both and seemed happy about it. Just before the crucifixion, a woman poured an expensive bottle of ointment on our Lord and was glad for the opportunity to do so. When the early church was in need, Barnabas sold his land and gave the money to the church, gladly. These are only a few of those mentioned who overcame the sin of unhappiness by freely saying, "All that I have is thine."

NOTES

1. Lewis Evans, *Your Marriage—Duel or Duet?* (Old Tappan, NJ: Fleming H. Revell Co., 1962), p. 86.

2. Howard Moody, *The Fourth Man* (New York: The Mac-Millan Co., 1964), p. 7.

3. Patsy Pritchett, "Illustrating the Sermon," quoting C. Neil Strait in *Proclaim 2* (October-December, 1971): 41.

4. J. Wallace Hamilton, *Horns and Haloes in Human Nature* (Old Tappan, NJ: Fleming H. Revell Co., 1954), p. 120.

5. Karl Olson, *Come to the Party* (Waco, TX: Word Books, 1972), pp. 27–52.

God is our refuge and strength,
a very present help in trouble.
(Ps. 46:1)

3

Deal with Your Loneliness

■In one of his songs, Harry Chapin says, "Yes I know I have a lifetime a-coming, but I got it all figured out; everybody's lonely, everybody's lonely, everybody's lonely. That's what it's all about."

In a joint discussion, psychiatrists Jean Rosenbaum, Natalie Shainers, and Antonio Wenkart agreed that loneliness is perhaps the most dangerous and widespread illness in our land. They felt loneliness had reached epidemic proportions, and was continuing to spread. They agreed that loneliness is now man's worst enemy. Dr. Rosenbaum observed: "Chronic loneliness nowadays affects from 75 to 90 percent of all Americans."[1] Loneliness, with its feelings of being unfulfilled, unloved, and surrounded by doubts and fears, causes people to do all kinds of destructive things.

Wade P. Huie, professor at Columbia Seminary, states:

> Loneliness is discovering that your parents are getting a divorce and you are being torn by a pull toward each parent. Loneliness is hearing the umpire call, "Strike three, you're out!" when the winning run is on third base. Loneliness is a college freshman, who is glad to be away from home, but who feels empty on the first day of classes. Loneliness is a six-year-old who does not know the name of any other first graders. Loneliness is a mother whose children are all away at school. . . . Loneliness is going to a party with friends and finding only the "chit-chat" and small talk of "dangling conversation.". . . Loneliness is growing old in a system that worships youth. Loneliness is lying on a hospital bed, looking at the ceiling, and asking, "How long? How long?" Loneliness is saying "no" when all the other girls say "yes." Loneliness is realizing that in some ways you can never go home again.[2]

Since loneliness affects all of us and is a major source of unhappiness, it is important that we learn how to deal with it.

CAUSES OF LONELINESS

The experience of separation begins at birth. Otto Rank believes the birth trauma to be the most crucial experience of all of life. Dr. Frederick Leboyer, a French obstetrician, has pioneered to minimize the shock of birth. He has worked to bring babies into the world smiling rather than crying, believing that as a result they will be emotionally healthier throughout their lives.[3]

But after birth, there are numerous causes of loneliness. They tend to fall into certain broad categories. The night before he was to meet his brother Esau, Jacob was lonely because he was plagued with guilt. Twenty years before he had cheated his own brother. Now that brother had to be faced, and Jacob was alone in his guilt. He not only wrestled with an angel, he also wrestled with himself and what he had become. He was a study in loneliness.

The prophet Hosea was lonely for a different reason. His wife had been untrue to him. She had betrayed his love. He was crushed—and lonely.

Grief is another cause of loneliness. When a loved one is taken in death the cloud of loneliness hangs over us. Mary and Martha, after their brother Lazarus died, mildly admonished the Lord when He came four days later. They said, "If thou hadst been here, our brother would not have died" (John 11:21).

Feelings of insecurity drive us to loneliness. Many of these feelings grow out of our competitive society, which fosters strife, envy, and jealousy. Although an outright failure makes us lonely, the mere fear of failure does the same. And most of our "growing up" experiences are marked by such insecurity. How well I remember the loneliness I felt on that first day I enrolled in high school, having just graduated from the eighth grade in a little country school. I can recall the loneliness I felt on those occasions when, as third baseman on the baseball team, I let hard ground balls pass between my legs into left field. In those situations, I felt entirely alone.

And so, failure or the fear of it, whether in achieving personal goals, in business, in marriage, or in any other area, shrouds us in loneliness. Indeed, anything that confronts us with our own limitations makes us silently cry out from our inner depths, "I wish I were dead!" We yearn for love and intimacy, but fear that if we allow another person into our lives, he will become a sort of Trojan horse from which we cannot protect ourselves. We fear being hurt.[4] This is why loneliness is sometimes less threatening than exposure. Someone stated the dilemma this way: "I'm so miserable without you, it is almost like having you around."[5]

So anything that confronts us with the harsh reality of the world, and particularly with its heartbreaks, causes us to be lonely. Anything that happens which forces us to give up part of the comfortable illusions with which we tend to surround ourselves makes us feel lonely. Henry Nouwen observes that each of us tends to create our own Disneyland where we can have everything safely under control. Therefore, any event which crashes into that make-believe world and forces us to acknowledge we are not God of the universe, threatens us and makes us lonely. Most of us can identify with the psalmist who said: "My heart is smitten, and withered like grass; so that I forget to eat my bread. . . . I watch, and am as a sparrow alone upon the housetop" (Ps. 102:4, 7).

WRONG RESPONSES TO LONELINESS

One can be immobilized by loneliness. He decides to simply give up on himself and everyone else. He reaches the depths of depression and gloom. He loses all zest for living. Life becomes a sentence pronounced upon him, a judgment which he must endure. The psalmist felt something of this as he said: "My tears have been my meat day and night, while they continually say unto me, where is thy God?" (Ps. 42:3). When Jacob thought his son Joseph had been killed by a wild animal, "All his sons and all his daughters rose up to comfort him; but he refused to be comforted; and he said, For I will go down into the grave unto my son mourning" (Gen. 37:35).

Edward Arlington Robinson describes the destructive results of loneliness in this poem:

> Whenever Richard Cory went downtown,
>   We people on the pavement looked at him.
> He was a gentleman from sole to crown,
>   Clean favored, and imperially slim.
> And he always was quietly arrayed,
>   And he was always human when he talked.
> But still he fluttered pulses when he said
>   'Good morning,' and he glittered when he
>   walked.
> And he was rich—yes, richer than a king.
>   And admirably schooled in every grace.
> In fine, we thought that he was everything
>   To make us wish we were in his place.
> So on we worked, and waited for the light,
>   And went without the meat, and cursed the
>   bread,
> And Richard Cory, one calm, summer night,
>   Went home and put a bullet through his
>   head.

One can become actively frantic. While some are immobilized by loneliness, others are driven to a mad search supposing that somewhere they can find another mate, another job, another experience that can bring escape from loneliness. They try to fill the void that is felt. Such people become workaholics, alcoholics, or sexually promiscuous in vain efforts to escape loneliness. The whole goal of the drug culture seems to be to escape the awful feelings of loneliness. But such an approach is doomed to failure.

THE USEFULNESS OF LONELINESS

Several years ago I went through a time of personal crisis as a pastor. I felt I was not fulfilling the high goals and lofty ambitions which I had nurtured deep within. Surrounded by loneliness, I went through some soul-searching experiences in which I had to face myself and, more important, face God and His will for my life. At last I was able to make peace with myself and with God about my calling. However, it was not until I read Henry Nouwen's book on loneliness, *Reaching Out*, that I was able to understand my own struggles and then help others deal with their problems with loneliness. I learned that there are some helpful suggestions and courses of action for lonely people. I am indebted to Nouwen's insight for much that follows.

Don't try to escape loneliness. To do so is to suppose you can cure yourself by filling the void with something temporary. No job, no person, no love, no attainment can heal your feelings of incompleteness. The belief that we can cure ourselves by any of these substitutes will lead us on a restless search throughout the rest of our lives.

Let loneliness lead you to solitude. Sören Kierkegaard, in *Sickness Unto Death*, notes with irony that the only use we have made of solitude is as a punishment for criminals—solitary confinement. In contrast, we need to discover the possibilities of solitude. And we can do this only if we recognize that loneliness can be looked upon as a *gift*, a means of inner discovery. A person has to be *alone* to make life's deepest discoveries. Rather than seek to escape loneliness, one must learn to allow it to lead him into solitude.

Solitude is peaceful. But the peace comes only when,

in the midst of loneliness, you decide to make peace between two people—yourself and God. When such peace is made you can enjoy being alone.

Start Therefore, use loneliness as a time to get acquainted with yourself all over again. As Hulme says, "There is a relationship of 'I' to 'me.' We can thus deceive ourselves, punish ourselves, forgive ourselves, or be good to ourselves."[6] The discovery of the self is as important as was Columbus' discovery of a new world. And such explorations are usually costly and painful.

When Jacob wrestled with God throughout that agonizing night, he was facing up to what he had become in the past twenty years. He was getting acquainted with himself all over again. He was trying to make peace with himself.

Jacob also got acquainted with God all over again. But this time he had to deal with God as God really is—not as Jacob had imagined Him. Since solitude (peace with oneself and with God) is the blessing toward which loneliness can lead, we need to take seriously the means by which we can arrive at such solitude—the means by which we can make peace with ourselves and with God.

THE TRANSITION FROM LONELINESS TO SOLITUDE

Our heavenly Father does not want us to be restless or lonely. With His help we can make the transition into solitude, peace with self and with Him, and discover life as it is meant to be. There are some simple steps which we must take, with God's help.

Dare to be totally honest. Do a thorough self-examination and lay everything out before God. Bolt all your inner doors; allow yourself no escape route. Search the attics of your mind and drag out all the guilt, fear, bitterness, hatred, and resentment. Ask God's forgiveness. Repent that you have harbored such things in your life and ask God to remove them. To fill your life with these bitter emotions is sin, and you need to ask forgiveness for such sin.

Accept God's forgiveness. Once sin has been confessed and earnest prayer has been made for God's forgiveness, accept that forgiveness. God's Word promises that if we have sincerely repented and confessed, He has forgiven. At this point we have to stop doing all the talking. We have to stop telling ourselves that we are still evil and bad and alienated from God. Kierkegaard, in *Sickness Unto Death*, says the only way out of despair is to realize the arms of God are there, unseen and outstretched. We must take the leap of faith into those arms which are open to accept us.

Sometimes, in order to accept the fact that God has forgiven you, it helps to find someone you can trust and confess to that person the same sins you have confessed to God. This involves a risk, of course. The friend could reject you. But if he is a real friend you will discover that he accepts you. This will help you to realize that God, too, has accepted you.[7]

Accept a new opinion of yourself. If God has accepted you, you can accept yourself. If He has forgiven you, you can forgive yourself. If God is not down on you it is wrong for you to be down on yourself. Robert Schuller reminds us that just as some people receive organ transplants, each of us needs a self-image transplant when we have made peace with ourselves and with God. He goes on to remind us that there is something every person needs more than anything else in life. The vital thing is not to survive, nor to experience pleasure, nor to have the feel of power, nor even to find meaning in life. Rather, the most sought-after need of every heart is to be able to have a genuine self-love. Self-love is not to be confused with selfishness nor the worship of one's self. Rather it has to do with being able to respect oneself, to enjoy being with oneself.[8] Connected with selflove is the will to dignity. For, when we give ourselves to God we become His children, and joint-heirs with Christ. Life has dignity to it and we have become a part of it. We are worth something at last, not because of our achievement, but because God has given us a self-worth.

Kierkegaard, in *Sickness Unto Death*, tells the story of a mighty emperor who sent for a poor laborer in his realm. The lad felt privileged to see the emperor, but when it turned out that emperor wanted him for a son-in-law the laborer was overwhelmed. This was too much! He could not accept such a position. He was not worthy! Such is our attitude toward God. We see ourselves as the day laborer in the presence of the King. Our self-esteem is so low we cannot accept the fullness of a position in the King's family.[9]

If you want to be able to accept a new image which God wants to give you, you must determine to be the kind of person who can be trusted, for we do not love those we cannot trust. You must determine to be the kind of person who gives love, for no one can respect someone else who never extends love. You must ever remind yourself that you are wanted and needed. You can do this by involving yourself in the problems of other people. You can respect yourself if you have become a helpful person. You can love yourself if you are true to the highest ideals and live by your convictions, so that you cease to be a phony. You dare to be what you know you ought to be. Since no one loves a coward, determine not to be cowardly. You do not have to succeed at everything you do, but you must be courageous.

In other words, determine to foster those characteristics which you respect, and then accept yourself, both physically, mentally, and emotionally, as you are. Everyone has limitations. Realize that God has chosen to work through you as you are, with whatever limitations you have. Also remember that God has not finished with you. He is still working in your life, and you are not yet all that you will be. No one is ever totally satisfied with himself. But if you have made peace with God, you can accept yourself. This will usher you into solitude, and deliver you from the spirit of restlessness. Solitude does not require sitting in a dark room all alone. Just as loneliness can occur in the midst of a great multitude of people, so can solitude. But solitude means that even when you are with people, you can be at peace with yourself, with them, and with God.

Accept a new vision of usefulness. I can remember moments when I felt utterly useless in my calling. When I got my doctorate in theology one of my children told a neighbor that I was the kind of doctor who could not help anyone.

I spent all one night in the hospital room of a policeman friend who had been brutally injured by a wild young man with a shotgun. The doctor and the nurses all seemed to be able to do something. It was quite apparent that the young physician, who was not a Christian, felt me to be very much in the way. There were times when I was asked to leave the room for certain periods. Finally, in the waning hours of the night, the dying man gained consciousness for a moment, though he could not speak. I stepped beside him, took his hand, and asked him if he were trusting himself in the hands of Christ. He answered with a warm, firm squeeze of my hand. I leaned over close to his ear and breathed aloud a soft prayer. Again he squeezed my hand. Suddenly I felt useful. Out of that experience I have realized that what the world needs above everything else is the presence of Christians to walk beside those in the pain of life and death.

My night had been interrupted by that tragedy, but I came to realize that interruptions are a vital part of my calling—perhaps the major part of my calling. It is so in the life of every Christian. God places us in this earth to minister in moments of interruptions and tragedies and loneliness. Our greatest contributions do not occur amid those things which we schedule, but amid those events that are unscheduled. And if we are wise, we discover that God has placed us where He has placed us because He knows what interruptions are going to occur.

Yield yourself to God's leading. Put aside all insecurities. God does not decree that we must succeed, but He does decree that we must be obedient. God will give us the power in our lives to do His will. Moses had been on the back side of the desert for forty years when one day, alone, he saw a bush burning without being consumed. God told him he had to return to the Egypt from which he had been expelled and lead the people from bondage. And so after forty years Moses became active again—he reentered life. After Jacob wrestled alone all night with God and with himself, he could face the sunrise, but more importantly, he could face his estranged brother. Out of that experience Jacob was given a new name—the name of Israel! God gives to each of us a new name, a new image, a new calling.

The Scriptures liken this calling to an inner, spiritual marriage covenant. A breach of this calling is depicted as spiritual adultery in the Old Testament. The same implication is found in the New Testament where the church is pictured as the bride of Christ. Thus our calling relates us to God, and to one another. No one is complete apart from this relationship. One does not have to marry another person to have a full life, but one must have a covenant commitment to Christ, or remain incomplete.[10]

Give yourself away. However, never assume that solitude means withdrawal from life. In an article, "The New Narcissism," Peter Marin points out the shortcomings and narcissism of such self-improvement programs as transcendental meditation. The danger is the deification of self at the expense of a concern for others. Self-denial and sacrifice for the benefit of others is central to the Christian calling. The Christ who came to die for us reminds us that to try to save our own life is to lose it. It is in the giving away of our life that we find ourselves.[11]

When you have used loneliness as a time to make peace with yourself and with God, thereby discovering solitude, you have actually made room in your soul for yourself and for God. The final step then is to make room in your life for others. Christ said that the secret to life is found not in saving it, but in giving it away. This is what discipleship is all about. Only a person at peace with himself and at peace with God can come to this understanding, to this spirit of giving that is the very basis of all discipleship. Just as no one can make you feel at home in his house unless he himself feels at home in it, no person can make others at home in their presence unless they are at home in their own presence.

The world is filled with lonely strangers who need to find someone who is willing to make room for them, to take time for them, to touch their lives. Even our children are guests who enter our home, stay for a while, and then set out on a journey of their own. Too often parents fail to make room for their children in their lives because they are not at peace with themselves. They have not discovered solitude. They are not able to give themselves away, even to their children.[12] Each of us as parents has to realize that since our children are but guests, we must make room for them, but we cannot look upon them as our possessions. We can try to prepare them for adulthood by allowing them a place in our lives, but we cannot assume responsibility for their lives. This they must do.

The problem with most marriages is that neither the husband nor the wife has found solitude, and therefore neither is able to give totally to the other. Lonely people shut themselves off from one another. Only those who have discovered solitude (peace with self and with God) are able to give of themselves.

Christ spent much time alone. He often withdrew from the crowds and from His disciples to spend time alone (John 6:15; Mark 1:35). Yet Jesus was never lonely in those moments. They were times of solitude. There was only one moment during which our Lord experienced loneliness. That moment was on the cross as He suffered in our place. It was there that He willingly chose to take upon Himself the sins of the world, and thus experienced separation from the Father. It is at this point we understand His cry from the cross: "My God, my God, why hast thou forsaken me?"

Yet it was in this moment of loneliness that our healing took place. It was in Christ's forsakenness that our wholeness became possible. This was the utter and total giving for which Christ became flesh. It is a moment that becomes our calling.

Each of us would do well to have a plaque on our wall like the one which reads: "Show me the person you want to speak to through my life today." The world is filled with lonely people to whom we are called to minister. Therefore when we find ourselves amid loneliness, we must remember that the goal is not to escape it, but to allow it to lead us into solitude—to a relationship of peace with self and with God. Loneliness will take you down a path; *you* can choose the path. You can determine that it lead you into solitude, and then from solitude out into the world with a feeling of self-worth, self-respect, self-love, and with the determination to give yourself away in His name.

NOTES

1. Keith Miller, *The Becomers* (Waco, TX: Word Books), pp. 32–33.

2. David MacLennan, "God and Our Loneliness," *Pulpit Digest* 52 (January, 1972): 39.

3. Wm. E. Hulme, *Creative Loneliness* (Minneapolis: Augsberg Press, 1977), pp. 24–25.

4. Hulme, p. 37.

5. Hulme, p. 80.

6. Hulme, pp. 50–51.

7. Robert Schuller, *Self-Love: The Dynamic Force of Success* (New York: Hawthorne Books, Inc., 1969), p. 100.

8. Schuller, pp. 18–21.

9. Hulme, pp. 38–39.

10. Hulme, pp. 68–69.

11. Hulme, pp. 100–101.

12. Henri J. M. Nouwen, *Reaching Out* (Garden City, NY: Doubleday, 1975), p. 56.

Let us love one another:
is of God. . . . for God
(I John 4.7 — 8)

4
Learn To Love

■An elderly man once shared with me his definition of love. It was simple: "Love is treating someone right." Without knowing it, he was very close to the definition given by psychiatrist Eric Fromm, who says that love is an attitude of respect, responsibility, and care, all coupled with the wish that the other person might grow and develop.[1]

Needless to say, there are different types of love. The Greek language, which in God's providence is the language of the New Testament, has three basic words for love, each depicting a different kind of love. Brotherly love (*phileo*) was used to speak of the warm love one had for his close friends and family.

The *eros* type of love is described in Plato's *Sym-*

posium as a primitive type of love much akin to sexual desire and marked by passionate craving, not only for physical beauty, but for beauty of mind and soul. Basically this kind of love is thought of as romantic love based on physical attraction. Although *eros* is not used in the New Testament, it was very much a part of the New Testament world as it is of our own world.

Inspired by the Holy Spirit, the New Testament writers selected a word for love, *agape*, which is only sparsely found in nonbiblical Greek literature. When it is found, it usually has a meaning such as "to be content with," "to like," "to esteem," "to prefer." It was this rather plain and colorless word that the translators of the Old Testament used when speaking of the love of God to man, and in turn, man's response to that divine love. Thus the Father chose to select a relatively unused and untainted word to describe His love, and then to fill that word with new and unique meanings so that it became distinctly Christian.[2]

This *agape* love came to be identified with the spirit of self-sacrifice whereby the good of others is sought, regardless of the cost involved. It is unselfish giving, regardless of the worth of the recipient. Only this kind of love can last, because if one's love is constantly based on the merit of the person loved, the very depravity of human nature will sooner or later cause that kind of love to cease. When we come to grips with *agape* love we are able to experience the other types of love as they were meant to be experienced.

One must learn how to love in three basic areas: God, others, and self. Since the Bible affirms that "God is love" (I John 4:8), we do well to begin our journey toward love by an examination of the way God loves us.

First let's be clear on what "God is love" means. In the New Testament, God is spoken of as "Spirit" (John 4:24) to help us understand that His unseen presence makes Him constantly available to each of us. He is described as "light" (I John 1:5), because He illuminates life in its proper perspective. However, the highest statement about God to be found in the New Testament is that "God is love." Keeping in mind that *agape* love is noted for its self-sacrifice and total giving, "God is love" means that everything God does is marked by sacrificial, total giving.

A LOOK AT HOW GOD LOVES

Before we deal with learning how to love God, we must learn about how He loves us.

With a love based on need. The amazing thing about God's love is that it is based on our need, not our merit. As human beings, we tend to love only those who deserve our love. In contrast, God loves us even when we do not deserve such love.

God often used the illustration of spiritual adultery to describe Israel's relationship to Him. Israel was a harlot who allowed her love to be disseminated, to be made common and vulgar. However, God never stopped loving her, and Israel the harlot was never forgotten. When all her other lovers had deserted her, God was there with His promise: "I will restore health unto thee, and I will heal thee of thy wounds" (Jer. 30:17).

When someone crosses a certain line, we are prone to say to them, "You don't deserve my love any longer." This may happen in a marriage relationship, between parent and child, or between friends. Let someone step across that line and commit a certain sin, bring about a certain disappointment, commit a certain offense, and they step beyond our love. But it is at that moment, when the whole world slams the door in a person's face, that God says, "But I still love you, not because you deserve it, but because you need it."

Our heavenly Father loves us as earthly parents love their children. For instance, when Adam and Eve sinned, God did not forsake them. When the world became so wicked that the judgment of the flood had to be sent upon it, God saved a family and started over again. He never gives up on us.

When the good Samaritan in Jesus' parable saw a Jewish man who had been beaten, robbed, and left to die alongside the road, he stopped and took care of the fellow, in spite of the racial prejudices that existed between their people. He helped because the man needed his help. The first thing, then, that we learn about God's love is that it comes because we need it.

With a love of endless dimensions. God's love is of such dimension that it "passes all understanding." Jeremiah reported God's love to the people: "The Lord hath appeared of old unto me, saying, Yea, I have loved thee with an everlasting love" (Jer. 31:3). The phrase, "the Lord hath appeared of old unto me," literally has the meaning, "as though from afar." Jeremiah used the word that means going as far as you can go only to discover that you have not even begun to exhaust the subject. For instance, you can go as far as you can go on the horizon, yet you haven't come to the end of the world.

With a wise love. Through Jeremiah God said, "I will correct thee in measure, and will not leave thee altogether unpunished" (Jer. 30:11). In the same chapter He said, "Behold the whirlwind of the Lord goeth forth with fury, a continuing whirlwind: it shall fall with pain upon the head of the wicked" (Jer. 30:23). God in His love must sometimes be stern. The storm of God has to sweep down and blow away all the things that clutter our lives. God is not some dotish parent who allows His children to run rampant without caring enough to correct them, without being wise enough to know what is not good for them. This is why God cast Adam and Even out of the Garden of Eden. He didn't hate them; He loved them and knew they had to understand what they had done. They had to experience loneliness before they could understand what it meant to be able to walk with God every day. God's storms are sometimes hard to understand. The Lord Himself tells us that it may be only the final days of life, or even of this earth, that at last bring an understanding of divine purposes (Jer. 30:24).

With a love that conquers all obstacles. The aspect of God's love that encourages us most is that His love overcomes, conquers, and showers us with hope. The Scriptures are an everlasting Word of hope because they give us a multitude of ways in which God loves us and is working in our lives to bring victory. Many things cause us to despair: We wonder about the future of our country, and indeed of the world, about economic policies, ecology, and world armaments. Amid all this, our hope is only in God and His love for us. The Christian faith has endured through the centuries, not because of leaders like Moses, prophets like Elijah, or apostles like Paul, but because of God—because of His power and grace and love.

The final triumph of God's love is found in Jesus Christ. God loved us enough to reveal Himself to us, to walk among us in human flesh. God's love "was made flesh and dwelt among us, (and we beheld his glory, the glory as of the only begotten of the Father), full of grace and truth" (John 1:14). "Herein is love, not that we loved God, but that he loved us, and sent his Son to bear the penalty for our sins" (I John 4:10, my translation).

We never fully understand God's love until we see Christ dying on the cross for our sins. This is the God of love who pursues us in order to redeem us. Over eighty years ago a Roman Catholic magazine printed a poem written by Francis Thompson. Two years before he wrote this poem, he was both a drunk and a drug addict. Then he surrendered to God's love in Christ and wrote his poem picturing God as one who pursued him as though a bloodhound. This was the story of his own conversion, of how he fled from God not knowing that it was in God he could find life. Those who first read it said it would never amount to anything because there was no poetry about it. Even after it was published it went unnoticed for some time. Then people began to discover in it a poetry of the soul. The poem has since been translated into sixty languages because it speaks to every man's heart who reads it. How vividly Thompson tells his experience: "I fled Him down the nights and down the days, I fled Him down the arches of the years; I fled Him down the labyrinthine ways of my own mind, and in the midst of tears I hid from Him. Halts by me that footfall, is my gloom after all merely the shade of His hand outstretched caressingly?"

Then he says, "Ah, fondest, blindest, weakest, I am he whom thou seekest." At last he had let God find him. He had stopped running and experienced the love of Christ which passes all understanding. Here lies the whole purpose of God's love: He wants to redeem us.

We must realize that God's love actually *does something* to us. John said that God's love is "perfected in us" (I John 4:12), signifying that His purpose is being accomplished in us.

God's love for us led to crucifixion of His only Son. Now His love gives us the ability to reproduce that same kind of sacrificial love. We will never be able to love completely until we allow God's love to enter our lives. As we learn to love God—respond to His love—we will learn to love others.

HOW TO LOVE GOD

Some have tried to depict man's love for God in terms that are sticky and sentimental. They even speak of putting their arms around God in embrace. What we must realize is that man shows his love for God in the same manner he shows his love for anyone else. The man who loves his wife shows it by doing things that please her; man shows his love for God by doing things that please Him. Jesus defined love for God in terms of obedience: "If ye love me, keep my commandments" (John 14:15). "He that hath my commandments, and keepeth them, he it is that loveth me: and he that loveth me shall be loved of my Father, and I will love him, and will manifest myself to him" (John 14:21). "If a man love me, he will keep my words, and my Father will love him and we will come unto him, and make our abode with him" (John 14:23). "He that loveth me not, keepeth not my sayings: and the word which you hear is not mine, but the Father's which sent me" (John 14:24).

If real love for God is evidenced by obedience to His

commandments, we must live according to divine guidelines. These guidelines relate not only to our love for God, but to our love for our fellow man. Only God knows what is best for our neighbor, what produces lasting joy. Left to ourselves, we are prone to look toward immediate and temporary benefits, for we have great difficulty in looking beyond the immediacy of our context.

Denying that we live in a time of moral crisis is blindness, as is supposing that we are facing the first moral crisis ever. For instance, read the following article:

> There is little doubt that the present generation of college young men and women is in serious moral difficulty. Compare it with the generations preceding; they have shunned discipline and a willingness to excel in their studies. Many give little or no thought to the serious issues of life. Common modesty and decency in manners and dress are apparently things of the past. The fact that evil is called good while good is called evil seems to be of small concern to them. Student groups indulge in wild orgies of self-gratification while co-eds dress and walk in a manner deliberately intended to arouse sexual desire. Both young men and women in their actions and conversation make sexual overtures in the most shameless fashion.[3]

The above paragraph seems as contemporary as tomorrow's newspaper headlines. Yet these words were written by the Greek dramatist, Aristophanes, in the fifth century B.C. This serves to remind us that Satan has always been close at hand. What is new today is that men are proclaiming a "new morality" which accepts behavior that the Ten Commandments have branded as sin.

Love of man, as divorced from love of God, is like a ship at sea without a compass and a rudder. If a man loves God by obeying God's commandments, he cannot genuinely love his neighbor by disobeying God's commandments. The holy commandments are not given merely for us, but also for the welfare of our neighbor.

Since God's Word labels homosexuality a perversion and a sin, we do a disservice to mankind if we approve it as a valid lifestyle. And since God has decreed that for a man and a woman to live together in a sexual relationship apart from marriage is a sin, we also do society an injustice if we approve that. Heartbreak comes to those who throw away God's moral laws. The dark ages of Israel came when, after the death of Joshua, the new generation decided to cast aside the laws of God and each became his own judge. The Scripture says of that generation, "Every man did that which was right in his own eyes" (Judg. 21:25). To cast aside God's morality is to live in rebellion against God, and thus set oneself up as God. There is nothing more frightening than a community of gods. Such a society would at last lead everyone to have the feelings expressed in Dorothy Parker's poem:

> There is little in taking or giving,
> There is little in water or wine,
> This living, this living, this living
> Was never a project of mine.
>
> Oh, hard is the struggle, and sparse is
> The gain of the one at the top,
> For art is a form of catharsis,
> And love is a permanent flop.
>
> And work is the province of cattle,
> And rest's for a clam in a shell,
> So I'm thinking of throwing the battle—
> Would you kindly direct me to hell?[4]

However, love is not synonymous with keeping God's laws. Faith, a response to God's laws that goes beyond rules, is our supreme expression of love for God. Marked by reverence and personal commitment, it is a surrender of our will to the will of the heavenly Father.

An incident in the life of Jesus provides insight into how we can live with God's laws, and at the same time live properly with His lordship in our lives. Jesus and His disciples were walking along a footpath between the long, narrow fields of Palestine on the Sabbath. Being hungry, the disciples plucked a few handfuls of wheat which they shelled with their hands and ate. The law stated that strangers were allowed to satisfy their immediate hunger as long as they did not use a sickle (Deut. 23:25). The issue of law breaking, in the eyes of the Pharisees, came about because the disciples plucked the wheat and rubbed it out in their hands. According to the Pharisees, the disciples were guilty of reaping, threshing, winnowing, and preparing a meal on the Sabbath.

Jesus answered the Pharisees' accusations with, "The Sabbath was made for man, and not man for the sabbath: therefore the Son of man is lord also of the Sabbath" (Mark 2:27—28). He directed the Pharisees to an incident in the life of David as a case in point. He reminded them that on one occasion David and some of his men, in need of food, requested the priest to give them the shewbread from the holy place. This shewbread (described in Leviticus 24:4—9) consisted of twelve loaves of bread which were placed each week outside the Holy of Holies. When the week was up, fresh bread was placed there, but only the priests could eat the replaced bread. These loaves of bread were a symbolic offering to God, thanking Him for the manna, the bread from heaven, which He provided during the wilderness wanderings of

Israel. The hunger of David and his men was more important than the law which forbade an ordinary man to eat the bread. Therefore David and his men ate and life was sustained. David was not condemned for that action, and Jesus reminded the Pharisees of that. Jesus was stressing that God is in the business of helping people, not in making laws.

When Jesus said, "The Sabbath was made for man, and not man for the Sabbath," He was saying that God's laws are for man's welfare. We must come to look upon God's laws as a gift. In our confusing world, the laws of God stand out to help us find direction, to give us insight into those things that are valuable, and to help us avoid those things that destroy.

The Sabbath serves as an illustration. Man needs desperately the gift of the Sabbath. Keeping the Sabbath does not necessarily mean that one has become godly, but it does provide an opportunity for spiritual dimensions, activities, and pursuits. A day apart from normal work and frustrations is a much-needed element for personal development and spiritual growth.

Legalism is an inefficient method of loving God, because it causes cold formality and false appearances. Legalism allows no love relationship to the living God. And when this relationship is missing, tension does not exist between what we are and what our Father wants to make us as it should. We must answer this: "What am I becoming?" To love God is to make progress in the direction of godliness.

Nathaniel Hawthorne based a story called, "The Celestial Railroad" on John Bunyan's *Pilgrim's Progress* in which he satirized the New England church of his day.

Whereas Bunyan pictured the Christian life in terms of a journey on which one must go through the Slough of Despond, the Iron Cage of Despair, the Battle with Satan, and so on, Hawthorne pictured the church life of his day in terms of a tourist attraction. The way between the City of Destruction and the Celestial City could be traveled in the railway car. For a small fee one could observe the Slough of Despond, the Iron Cage of Despair, and the Battle with Apollyon as a tourist, an onlooker. Thus for a small sum of money, one could say he had made the trip, yet experience no danger, and no change in his life at all.

Christian psychologist, Wayne Oates, finds this tourist role a very great danger in our present religious milieu. It is easy to make conversion nothing more than the acceptance of certain rules and the performance of certain acts, making it possible to take the name of Christian without any real risk, or without really engaging in the battle with the forces of evil.[5]

Alan Redpath tells about an experience in 1951 when twenty-four leaders of the China Inland Mission Overseas Missionary Fellowship met together in Manila in the face of a great crisis. They had been forced out of China and were concerned about their next move. There seemed to be no sense of divine direction. One day, by invitation, there entered that conference the last surviving daughter of General Booth. As she listened to their conversations she suddenly interrupted: "Gentlemen, how do you spell love?" When they responded with the usual spelling, she replied, "No, gentlemen. Will you allow me to spell love for you? It is spelled s-a-c-r-i-f-i-c-e."[6] We love God by living out faith that is willing to sacrifice.

HOW TO LOVE YOURSELF

As mentioned earlier, we have to learn to love in three areas. We must learn to love God, self, and others. Once we have learned what it means to love God, the next step is to come to grips with what is involved in loving oneself.

I preached many sermons concerning our need to love God, and to love our neighbors, before it occurred to me that Scripture also admonishes a person to love himself: "Thou shalt love thy neighbor *as thyself*" (Matt. 22:39, italics mine). Fromm reminds us that we are the object of our own feelings and attitudes just as others are. He says: "From this it follows that my own self, in principle, must be an object of my love as another person. The affirmation of one's own life, happiness, growth, freedom, is rooted in one's capacity to love, i.e., in care, respect, responsibility and knowledge. If an individual is able to love productively, he loves himself too; if he can love only others, he cannot love at all."[7]

God tells us that in marriage a man and woman become as one, and He admonishes the man to love his wife as he does his own self. Scripture (Eph. 5:28) goes on to say that no man ever hated himself. Even in suicide a man does not hate himself, but is trying somehow to draw attention to himself or shelter himself from further suffering. Though a man does not purposefully hate himself, he may have never learned to love himself.

Have you ever paused to contemplate whether or not you treat yourself right? There are multitudes of miserable people who have never learned how to love themselves. In fact, many have even supposed that they were expected to hate themselves in order to love others.

We are not to confuse self-love with narcissism which is a term coined by Freud to speak of neurotic self-love, based on the Greek myth of Narcissus who was a beautiful youth, but was incapable of loving anyone else. He worshiped his own image which he saw in a pool of water and could never really take his eyes off himself. Real love for self is built around the concept that love is treating yourself right. Let's see what this involves.

Be honest with yourself. How often has a wife said to her husband, "You don't love me, or you would not lie to me." There is a great truth here: We do not lie to those we love. The same truth is applicable in learning to love yourself. Many of the parables Jesus used were to help people see themselves as they really were. When Jesus spoke with a woman of Samaria in the middle of the day at the well just outside town, He led the discussion in such a way that she saw herself in full honesty. As she went running back to town she exclaimed to those nearby, "He told me all things that ever I did." What is even greater, is that she recognized all the things she had done.

One of the best ways of knowing where you are heading is to take a look at where you have been. If avid social drinkers would take a look at where they have been, they would recognize that unless something changes they will be alcoholics in a few years. And young people experimenting with drugs or sex would see that they are heading for emptiness and loss of self-respect. It is strange that we who drive automobiles with warning lights to show us if the oil pressure drops, who watch blast-offs that sometimes are halted because warning lights come on, still refuse to acknowledge the warning light that God has given each of us—the conscience. Drakeford tells that "conscience makes us into real persons, capable of reaching untold possibilities."[8] Apart from a basic core of convictions true to one's conscience, there is no center to one's personality.

Confession comes when we decide to drop the sham. If we love ourselves we will stop worrying about saving face and confess. The poet writes:

> Is always a mask
> Held in the slim hand, whitely,
> Always she had a mask before her face—
> Smiling and spritely,
> The mask.
>
> For years and years I wondered
> But dared not ask
> And then—
> I blundered,
> I looked behind the mask,
> To find
> Nothing—
> She had no face.
>
> She had become
> Merely a hand
> Holding a mask
> With grace.[9]

Confession is not self-abnegation but the beginning of self-fulfillment—the beginning of treating yourself right. Apart from this honesty, life drifts into nothingness as depicted by the girl who in April, 1969, was found in a trance in a Las Vegas hotel, bound with adhesive. She was unable to remember what had happened. When asked her name, she said, "Eno Onmai." Someone at last discovered that these two meaningless words, when turned backwards, read, "I am no one."

Discipline yourself. Another aspect of treating yourself

right—of loving yourself—is discipline. Have you not seen a rebellious child who seemed determined to destroy everything he touched, and said to yourself, "If his mother loved him, she would discipline him"? The same is true in learning to love yourself. You can either love yourself enough to discipline yourself, or you can spoil yourself rotten.

Scripture tells us that we are to love God with all that we are. Confession opens our lives to this allegiance and discipline sees that we carry it out. In this way we are delivered from belonging only to ourselves. Years ago a man tried to assassinate President Franklin Roosevelt. One of the questions asked of the assassin was whether or not he belonged to a church. He answered, "No, no, I belong only to myself, and I suffer."[10]

Jesus warned against being overly dependent upon members of one's family. His words have often been misunderstood: "If any man come to me, and hate not his father, and mother, and wife, and children, and brethren, and sisters, yea, and his own life also, he cannot be my disciple" (Luke 14:26). Jesus is trying to help us understand that to be His disciples, to place our allegiance in Him, we are not to remain in a perennial childhood of dependence on, or allegiance to, others. The idea of "hate" used in this Scripture is best translated "disowning" or "renouncing." We are to reject, as far as allegiance is concerned, the natural and legal ties of family. God's will must come first.

We must never confuse self-love with selfishness. The two may seem to be identical on the surface, but they are actually opposites. To quote Fromm, "The selfish person does not love himself too much but too little; in fact, he hates himself. It is true that selfish persons are incapable of loving others, but they are not capable of loving themselves either."[11]

The words of Jesus about hating the members of one's family are concluded by the admonition that one must hate his own life also in order to be a disciple. At first this seems to be contradictory to the concept of loving yourself. But Jesus is saying that we must say, "no" to self-worship, to allegiance to oneself. Saying "no" to one's life is saying, "no" to a doomed life. We are at the same time saying, "yes," to the life God wants to give us, and to eternity.

Part of the discipline of love demands that we assume responsibility. Those who are helping people find themselves are discovering through various types of "integrity therapy" that irresponsibility makes neurotics of many people. If you love yourself you will compel yourself to assume responsibility for your actions and for your decisions.

One of the most successful techniques in recent times for treating drug addicts is based on the patient's willingness to assume responsibility for his addiction. At Day Top Village, a drug addict is treated not as an ill patient, but as a person who has been irresponsible.

To begin with, an addict who wants to enter Day Top is given enough money for his ferry and bus fare. It is up to him to arrive at his destination. From the time he arrives he is told by the workers, all of whom are cured addicts, that he has been living like a child, and if he is to enter the program he must grow up and accept responsibility.

Provide your needs. Part of loving ourselves is providing for our needs. We need food, clothing, time to ourselves, vacations, friends, and hobbies. But more importantly, we have spiritual needs—the need to be loved, and the need to love. Of utmost importance is a willingness to allow God to love us. Thielicke says man is like a photographic plate that can be immersed in a number of developing fluids which in turn produce different quality pictures. He says the real image of man can emerge only when immersed in the love of God.[12]

Man's search for wholeness is a spiritual quest. He needs the assurance that there is beyond him a heavenly Father who loves him and watches over him. He needs the peace that comes from forgiveness. "Realized forgiveness," to use Emerson's words, often comes by making restitution for things we have done that are wrong.

When Zacchaeus was converted, he said he would restore fourfold money he had taken dishonestly from people. Because he could not make everything right, he then said that half of his goods would be given to the poor. He realized he was beginning a new life, and it was this action that allowed him to go home that day with "realized forgiveness."[13]

One of our basic needs is a plan for the future. A man doesn't love his wife if he makes no plans at all for her future. Neither does he love himself if his future is ignored. When Jesus said we are not to be anxious about tomorrow, He was speaking of faithless anxiety. He expects us to be ready for eternity.

Respect yourself. When you can respect yourself, you can enjoy life day by day. The apostle John proclaimed, "Now are we the sons of God." Those who fail to respect themselves try a number of options. In fact, twenty-five thousand Americans each year commit suicide and other thousands try. Others destroy themselves piecemeal by drugs or drink. Some try selfish rebellion. Some have the attitude, "If I can't have what I want, I will see to it that no one else has it either." The great increase in crime is in part due to this way of thinking. Another alternative is self-resignation or blind submission. A person yields to the status quo, saying, "What is to be will be." Such a person wallows in self-pity and his will collapses.

The Christian's answer to self-acceptance is, as the apostle Paul said, "I can do all things through Christ." Reinhold Niebuhr's famous prayer has this theme: "God grant me the serenity to accept the things I cannot change, the courage to change the things I can, and the wisdom to distinguish the one from the other."

After we have confessed our failures, we are not to brood over them. We must determine to see the vision of light that God casts on our path, to see our good side. To love ourselves in this fashion, is to throw away all false humility, recognize our virtues, and use them.

Centuries ago a man named Bernard of Clairvaux wrote a sermon on love in which he said there are four levels: 1) First is the level where you love self for self's sake. This is much like a baby who sees only himself. 2) Then you come to the place where you love your neighbor for self's sake just as a baby loves his mother because his mother feeds him. 3) Next you progress to the stage where you love God for self's sake because you have discovered it is advantageous to love God. 4) The last stage is where you decide to love self all over again, for God's sake. This is the healthy self-love of which we have spoken. Love is the most powerful force in the world, and we must never suppose that we are to live without loving ourselves. As the French theologian Pierre Teilhard de Chardin said, "Some day, after mastering the winds, the waves, the tides and gravity, we shall harness for God the energies of love. And then, for the second time in the history of the world, man will discover fire!''[14]

HOW TO LOVE OTHERS

Keep in mind the three areas where we must learn to love—God, self, and others. It is impossible to really love others in a healthy way until we have first learned to love God and then to love self.

Loving others does not necessarily mean we will like others. Some people we can never really like because of a conflict in personalities. However, as Christians we are admonished to love all people—to treat them right.

Scripture tells us that one test of Christianity is the test of love: "If we love one another, God dwelleth in us, and His love is perfected in us" (I John 4:12). The growth of God's love in our own lives, with the passing of time, allows us to make progress in our ability to love others.

Simon Peter was once led to the house of a Gentile named Cornelius where he saw that household genuinely accept Christ as Lord. For Simon Peter to accept Cornelius as a Christian brother, was to go across the grain of everything he had been taught concerning the hated Gentiles. But because God's love had lodged in his heart, he recognized that he must either accept these Gentiles as brothers in Christ, or engage in a personal battle with the living God (Acts 11:17).

Few things tell us more about a man than does his willingness to love others. Plutarch once said that love for others seemed to be one of the secrets of Christian morality. He noted that the keynote of Christian love was never in terms of self-protection, but of self-giving to help others. This was directly opposite of the outlook of the Stoic who always emphasized self and explored every means of protecting self from all emotions or outward problems that would disturb inner tranquility.

In New Testament days, certain pagan religions led men to believe that they could see God through mystic rites and dramas. In contrast, the Scripture affirms that men are able to see God, first in Jesus Christ, and secondly in the way Christians love one another. An American journalist serving in China watched while a Catholic sister cleansed the gangrenous wounds of hospitalized soldiers. The journalist said to her, "I wouldn't do that for a million dollars." Without pausing, the sister replied, "Neither would I."[15] It was her way of saying that only God's love can lead to such self-giving.

It is at the point of loving others, of treating others right, that the golden rule comes into play: "Therefore all things whatsoever ye would that men should do to you, do ye even so to them: for this is the law and the prophets" (Matt. 7:12). Others before Christ had made similar statements, but always in a negative fashion. Confucius once said, "What you do not want done to yourself, do not do to others." The Stoic philosopher Epictetus said, "What you avoid suffering yourselves, seek not to inflict upon others."

Inaction can satisfy the negative form of the golden rule. One can stay in bed, pull the covers up over his head, and keep the golden rule. But Christ's golden rule indicates we must go out of our way to help others, to be gracious and kind to them, just as we would appreciate others going out of their way to help us.

If you want to know how to love others, ask yourself:

"How do I wish to be treated by others? What are my basic needs in human relations?" Do not we all wish for respect, fair play, genuine concern, friendship and warmth, a helping hand in time of trials?

The golden rule would destroy cliques if practiced among young people. Several years ago I visited with a young person whose clothing was not of the latest style and who was somewhat overweight. She told me she attended our church one time and had a very unhappy experience. In her Sunday school class, the "in crowd" sat on one side of the room, and she sat alone on the other side. Some very unkind remarks about her parents were made loudly enough that she could hear them. She had never been back. Whether in church or in school, this happens day in and day out.

Most adults know little about the golden rule. In our society we still see people as "haves" or "have-nots." We see people in terms of their social positions or the color of their skin. Our social and racial problems exist in horrendous proportion today because of neglect of the golden rule.

Abraham Lincoln was able to look beyond the insults of people and see them as they really were. Edwin M. Stanton, Lincoln's secretary of war, once referred to Lincoln as "this great ignoramus from Illinois, a baboon who doesn't have brains enough to be president." Yet Lincoln kept Stanton in office because he felt Stanton was the best secretary of war the nation had ever had. The words on Lincoln's tomb in Springfield, "Now he belongs to the ages," came from the lips of Stanton after Lincoln's death. Even Stanton realized the greatness of the man. The golden rule insists that we treat people right.

If husbands and wives lived by the golden rule, the

divorce rate would become nil. There is an ancient legend about two knights, each of whom was traveling in full battle regalia. In the darkness of the night they suddenly confronted one another. Each had supposed himself to be the only person for miles, so each was startled. Since the first reactions were those of fright, each interpreted the other as preparing for attack. Immediately they began to joust, each supposing he was defending himself against some awesome enemy. At last one unhorsed the other, driving his stake through the heart. Dismounting, the victor walked back and pulled open the faceguard of the knight he had just killed only to discover, to his horror, that the frightening stranger had indeed been his younger brother. How often marriages operate by reflex action, each spouse supposing the other to be hostile until a battle develops, leaving one mortally wounded emotionally and spiritually.

If the golden rule were practiced by all in parent-child relationships, there would be few rebels and few runaways. In an interview on a radio program, a man and his wife, both blind, told of the joy brought to their lives just from their own baby's smile. When asked how the couple knew the baby smiled at them, they replied that, while they could not see the smile, they sent their love out to the baby and could feel it coming back. Therefore they were certain the baby was smiling—as certain as if they could see it with their own eyes. Extended love has a way of being returned.

The highest goal in life is to treat others as every human being needs to be treated, recognizing they also are loved by the heavenly Father. Maxwell Anderson's play, *The Wingless Victory*, is the story of a sea captain from Salem, Massachusetts, who brought his new bride, a beautiful

Malaysian princess, back to his home in eighteenth-century New England. The princess tried in every way to adapt to her new surroundings. She accepted the Christian religion, learned the English language, became acquainted with the mores of American living, yet in everything she did she was rejected and ostracized merely because she was a brown-skinned person in a white society. At last, defeated in spirit, she returned to her homeland taking her two children with her. Standing on the deck of the ship as the American continent disappeared in the distance, she said: "He came too soon, this wonderful Christ of peace. It is beautiful—His vision that all human beings are brothers and sisters to each other. But the world does not seem ready for such a vision yet. Perhaps in another hundred thousand years they will listen, but not now."

However, it is important to keep in mind that the golden rule is not a religion. The person who bypasses Jesus Christ with the excuse that His is a "religion of the golden rule," has not begun to understand what Christ said. The golden rule is not a religion, but rather is an outgrowth of a conversion experience, of genuinely loving Christ.

Not only is the golden rule exclusively Christian, it can be applied only in the Christian context. If, for instance, you were one of two men left on a sinking ship, with only one place left in the lifeboat, and the other man insisted you take that one place, you would feel an eternal sense of obligation to him. Suppose, as the lifeboat pulled away, he called out to you asking that you "do as much for somebody else." This is the context in which we must interpret the golden rule. Christ took our place on the cross, died for our sins, and now bids us concern ourselves with others in the same spirit of self-sacrifice and graciousness.[16] What we find, then, is that the golden rule can practically be equated with Jesus' command to "love thy neighbor as thyself."

Bruce Larson tells about the time he was riding a motorcycle in the midst of heavy traffic with cars all around him, when suddenly a wasp flew into the open neck of his shirt. Although Larson was experiencing the painful sting of the wasp, he maintained a facade of normalcy. He pretended nothing was happening. He didn't want to panic or to cause an accident. He didn't want to look ridiculous. He continued to ride along looking peaceful and unperturbed. By the time he was able to work himself out of the traffic and take off his shirt he had six wasp stings. Out of that experience he observes that all around us are people who have wasps in their shirts, yet choose to pretend that nothing is wrong. They don't want to be embarrassed by admitting that they have a problem. He suggests that in every congregation, in every worship service, there are people who are looking placid and peaceful while, in reality, the wasps are stinging their hearts. Some have been dishonest, some have cheated on their spouses, some are suffering the pangs of guilt for sins never repented of—the list is endless.[17] These are the people all about us whom we must learn to love.

Although our first impression may be to fear such total love, Scripture reassures us by saying: "Herein is our love made perfect, that we may have boldness in the day of judgment . . . . There is no fear in love; but perfect love casteth out fear: because fear hath torment. He that feareth is not made perfect in love" (I John 4:17–18). In this passage, "fear" is accompanied with a definite article which, in the Greek language, means that a specific kind of fear is in question. The remainder of the verse explains the particular fear with which John is dealing—fear of the judgment. As love matures (God's kind of love in us), it will gradually cast out all fear of the final day when we shall stand before Him.

By learning to love God, and to love one another, we need have no agonizing worries about being called to give an account for life. Love will not keep house along with bitterness, selfishness, hatred, or fear. The degree to which one casts out these evil roommates becomes an accurate measure of one's love.

The love of which we have spoken does not come naturally: We learn to love. Indeed we may have to force ourselves to love, but if we do it often enough, we will discover that it does begin to come naturally by the help of Christ. One thing is certain, we shall never outgrow our need for love: "And now abideth, faith, hope, and love, these three, but the greatest of these is love" (I Cor. 13:13).

NOTES

1. Eric Fromm, *Man for Himself* (New York: Fawcett World Library, 1947), p. 110.
2. C. H. Dodd, *The Johannine Epistles* (New York: Harper and Brothers, 1946), pp. 110–12.
3. Aristophanes, "The Clouds," *Eight Great Comedies,* Sylvan Barnet, ed. (New York: New American Library of World Literature, 1958), pp. 48–49.
4. Dorothy Parker, "Coda," *Not So Deep As a Well, Collected Poems of Dorothy Parker* (New York: Viking Press, 1936), p. 149.
5. Wayne E. Oates, *The Psychology of Religion* (Waco, TX: Word Books, 1973), pp. 105–106.

6. Alan Redpath, *The Royal Route to Heaven* (New York: Fleming H. Revell Co., 1960), p. 171.

7. Fromm, pp. 134–35.

8. John W. Drakeford, *Integrity Therapy* (Nashville: Broadman Press, 1967), p. 15.

9. Helen Joseph, "The Mask," *Saturday Review*, August 13, 1932, quoted in Drakeford's *Integrity Therapy*, pp. 86–87.

10. Eugene Bay, "On Not Being Defeated by Life," *Reader's Digest* 97 (February, 1969): 26.

11. Fromm, pp. 135–36.

12. Helmut Thielicke, *Are You Nobody?* (Richmond, VA: John Knox Press, 1968), p. 46.

13. Drakeford, p. 64.

14. John Reddy, "The School That Love Built," *Reader's Digest* 99 (September, 1971): 154.

15. *The Interpreter's Bible*, George Buttrick, ed. (New York: Abingdon Press, 1957) XII: 281.

16. George Buttrick, "Discipleship and the Golden Rule" *Pulpit Digest* 46 (January, 1966): 20.

17. Bruce Larson, *The Relational Revolution* (Waco, TX: Word Books, 1976), p. 72.

For if ye forgive men
their trespasses,
your heavenly Father
will also forgive you.
(Matt. 6:14)

5

Participate in Forgiveness

■The growth of our souls will forever be malignant unless
we have the antidote of forgiveness. A full life cannot
begin until forgiveness is received, and cannot continue
until forgiveness is granted. However, genuine forgiveness is a costly item—both to the forgiver and the forgiven. Forgiveness is one of the great needs of our world.

The Greek word for forgiveness literally means to send
something away so that it is no longer present, no longer
in effect. In the papyri, the word was used in connection
with canceling some legal obligation, such as a debt.
Other times it was used by the courts in granting pardons.
It is used in the Septuagint where it sometimes means "to
leave in peace" (Judg. 2:23), or "to remit sin and guilt"
(Isa. 58:6; 61:1). When God forgives our sins, He in

effect sends them away, excluding them from His consideration of our case.

Jesus once told the story of a king who, out of compassion, forgave the large debt of one of his servants. But the forgiven servant, confronting a fellow-servant who owed *him* money, was not willing to forgive the debt and straightway had the poor fellow thrown in jail (Matt. 18:21–35).

When word of the cruel action reached the ears of the king, he was so angered that he turned his servant over to the authorities also. "Those who will not forgive will not be forgiven," says Jesus. To forgive a debt is to give up what is legally due you. To forgive an offense against you is willingly to give up resentment, along with all claims to restitution.

To understand forgiveness, we must look at it from two vantage points—the divine and the human, the forgiver and the forgiven.

RECEIVING FORGIVENESS

The age-old question pursues each of us: "How am I to deal with my sins?" We find ourselves living in regret about past failures and mistakes. We are confronted by the truth of the poet who wrote: "The moving finger writes, and having writ moves on; Nor all your piety nor wit can lure it back to cancel half a line, Nor all your tears wash out a word of it." What then are we to do?

The human involvement. The Bible has much to say about our feelings of grief and guilt that result from wrongdoing. Two perspectives of grief are mentioned in Scripture (II Cor. 7:9–11). There is the world's outlook on grief, and there is God's outlook on grief. There is the world's solution and there is God's solution. The world's perspective of grief leads one to regret (*metamelomai*). God's perspective of grief leads one to repent (*metanoeo*). The world's regret leaves one in his sins and leads to spiritual death. The godly grief that leads one to repentance brings salvation, forgiveness, and peace.

The difference between the world's outlook on grief and God's outlook on grief is the difference between death and life. Worldly regret effects no cure at all, but godly sorrow is the pathway to repentance and peace. This means there are times when we need to ask ourselves, "What do these tears mean?" Following the betrayal of Jesus, Judas recognized his sin and amid the dark clouds of his deep regret went out and hanged himself. In contrast, others who took part in the crucifixion of Jesus repented on the day of Pentecost and found a new life. Let us examine more carefully the two basic alternatives for dealing with sin.

The worldly grief (*metamelomai*) mentioned in Scripture means merely to regret something. It includes feelings of worry and anxiety about the fact that we have done something wrong. This kind of regret can bring on the despair pictured by George Eliot who wrote to a friend, "My address is Grief Castle." There are certain broad categories which describe the way our world, apart from God, tries to deal with its sins.

Blame others. In an effort to avoid depression and regret there are those who have refused to accept any blame themselves. Personal failures are always someone else's fault. In effect, this becomes a kind of "no-fault" theology, similar to the no-fault casualty insurance, where no one is legally to blame in an accident. The noted psychiatrist, Karl Meninger, sees this as one of the major problems of our time. He notes that our society has announced that sin has ceased to be. Thus the only solutions to be found involve treating neurotics and punishing criminals.[1]

Anna Russell has written a modern folk song that depicts this kind of attitude so prevalent with us today:

I went to my psychiatrist to be psychoanalyzed
To find out why I killed the cat and blacked my
    husband's eyes.
He laid me on a downy cough to see what he could find,
And here is what he dredged up from my subconscious
    mind:

When I was one, my mommy hid my dolly in a trunk,
And so it follows naturally that I am always drunk.
When I was two, I saw my father kiss the maid one day,
And that is why I suffer now from kleptomania.

At three, I had the feeling of ambivalence toward my
    brothers,
And so it follows naturally I poisoned all my lovers.
But I am happy; now I've learned the lesson this has
    taught;
That everything I do that's wrong is someone else's fault.[2]

I do not mean to discount the value of psychiatry. I have often suggested that people see a psychiatrist. However, for many today, psychiatry has become a kind of religion, and the psychiatrist has become a priest. We should never suppose that psychiatry is intended as an answer for our sins. Psychiatry may help us face our problems but it is no substitute for the gospel that speaks of repentance. Also, one must keep in mind that there are many different approaches in psychiatry. Only those which are consistent with the scriptural framework can prove helpful.

Dr. Jay Adams facetiously illustrates the differences between various counseling approaches with a simple parable. He pictures a poor man sitting on a tack and suffering from severe pain. A counselor who uses the somatic or chemical viewpoint surveys the situation and prescribes tranquilizers or pain killers. A surgical specialist comes by and suggests that the nerves which are activated should be severed. This will blot out the symptoms and give the client relief. A Freudian analyst looks over the situation and prescribes hours of sessions wherein the patient's childhood experiences can be delved into, particularly his early sexual experiences. Next a Rogerian counselor appears and refuses to give any advice at all. His solution is merely to listen to the problems of the man sitting on the tack and then reflect and restate his problems back to him that he may gain further insight. What the poor man needs is a counselor to come along who will tell him to get off the tack and will help him devise ways to avoid sitting on tacks in the future.[3]

Apologize. For some people the solution to everything is an eloquent apology. There is no question that an apology has its place. Yet we must never fall into the pattern of supposing that where our relationship to God is concerned, where our sins against Him are concerned, that an apology is effective.

The problem with an apology is that it usually lists some precise incident and deals with it as an isolated event, ignoring every other aspect of conduct. There is a certain security involved in an apology because once it has been made, then the other person must grant forgiveness or he is involved in sin. Therefore apology provides a kind of "legal way out" of one's problems.

One who apologizes will often spend as much time justifying what he has done as he will apologizing for it. In contrast to an apology, repentance is a shattering admission of guilt. Repentance makes no attempt to justify oneself, nor does it demand an easy forgiveness. Repentance merely throws itself on the mercy of the court.

Suppose, for instance, that someone borrows your best suit of clothes and proceeds to wear it on a hiking trip through thick underbrush. Each time he snags your coat he pauses to apologize. When he drags your shoes through the thorn thickets he apologizes for the deep gashes left on the leather. After a while his apologies begin to wear thin, along with your patience. As long as he keeps hiking through the underbrush he will continue to repeat his mistakes. It is not the individual incidents that need to be apologized for; rather, his whole direction must be changed. He must stop hiking in your best suit. Apologies are insufficient.

Make restitution. There are many fine people who regret their sinful action, and determine to make things right, to make restitution. This is a noble and good response. The Bible itself indicates that restitution should be made when wrongs are committed. The problem is that restitution is often impossible. We do not have the privilege of living past events over again.

Esau wept after he sold his birthright for a mess of pottage. Yet Scripture says that he found no way of setting the matter straight. What was done was done (Heb. 12:17). When King David took for himself the wife of Uriah, he secretly ordered that Uriah be placed in the front lines of the battle that he might be killed. When

God's Spirit confronted David with his guilt there was no way he could make restitution. A life had been snuffed out. I saw a man weep uncontrollably one day because during the war he had operated a machine gun and had seen men killed because of his action. There was no way he could ever make restitution.

The world's way of dealing with grief leaves us to ourselves and makes of life a long series of regrets, of repeat performances, of crushing burdens of guilt, of endless depression and sorrow for which there seems to be no relief. Too often we are like the little girl who was able to ride her bicycle, but not able to stop it. She had to keep going around the block until she met someone who would seize the handlebars and stop her. By ourselves, we cannot stop the vicious cycle of sin and regret. It is at this point that God's way of dealing with our failures and sins comes into focus.

Repentance (*metanoeo*) means more than regret; it is a complete change in one's values, disposition, and will. It is a complete reversal of one's whole direction in life. The literal meaning of the word is "to change one's mind." God is able to use our regrets to lead us to this kind of total repentance. For this reason Jeremy Taylor once said, "Godly sorrow is the porch that leads to repentance." Repentance does not merely look back with regret and fear, it is also able to look ahead in hope and anticipation. Salvation is an experience with God whereby a man becomes "a new creation" (II Cor. 5:17). It is spoken of as being "born from above" (John 3). God's way of dealing with our sins is to open up a new future for us by making us new people.

When one repents (changes his total mind and outlook), he realizes that there are not merely a few things wrong, but that his whole direction in life is wrong. He at last begins to understand what Jesus had in mind when He said, "What shall it profit a man if he gain the whole world, and lose his own soul?"

Since repentance involves a change of mind, one's present outlook and will must be totally surrendered. No longer does one seek to justify his behavior. Rather, he is willing to accept his guilt and his sinfulness along with the possibility that God can work a radical change in his life. To surrender one's will involves a struggle as deep as the soul itself.

The real issue in repentance is whether or not one hates his sin because he recognizes it as opposition to the will of God, or whether he merely hates his sin because of the pain it has caused.

Scripture reminds us that "there is a way that seemeth right unto man, but the end thereof is the way of death" (Prov. 14:12). There are times when, like an automobile, we have to back up and turn around. We come to dead-end streets. Genuine repentance not only involves turning around, it also involves the acceptance of God's revelation in the Scriptures as to which direction one should take. It is not enough to agree that God's way is the best. There must come with the turning around a whole-hearted, enthusiastic approval of God's way.

When one turns from his own direction in life to accept God's direction, he is in reality turning from himself to face the living God. At this point he is ready to ask forgiveness and receive God's gift of salvation. Conversion is something that happens to us by virtue of the power of God as we turn in repentance, asking forgiveness. It is then that peace and healing can take place.

While we need to make full restitution for our sins, wherever possible, we must realize that there can be healing for those things for which restitution is impossible. Whether this involves events which cannot be relived, whether it involves guilt feelings about the death of a loved one, whether it involves broken homes or automobile accidents which have taken the lives of loved ones, a healing can take place. As we confess our sins, God removes the burden of guilt from our shoulders. He fills us with a peace we never thought possible. When He forgives us He separates our sins from us as far as the east is from the west.

However, even after he accepts forgiveness in Christ, the Christian still gets off course. In those moments the Holy Spirit will speak to him, and he will turn, retrace his steps, repent, and come back to his commitment to Jesus Christ.

While the initial act of receiving forgiveness through faith in Christ involves a totality of life, there follows the day-by-day problem of dealing with continued acts of wrongdoing which bring us guilt and unhappiness. At this point confession of sin must be very specific. No longer is it possible to pray a blanket prayer of confession that says, "Forgive me of all my sins."

Confessional churches affirm that once a sin has been openly confessed, together with proper penance and restitution, one is never to bring that particular sin again to the confessional time. The truth behind this practice concerns the finality of God's forgiveness. Once we have brought a sin to God in confession we have to realize that the matter is closed. God's forgiveness is permanent. Since forgiveness is something that actually happens, it becomes as real as the sin. We must learn to accept the fact that God's forgiveness is not merely some legal paperwork, but is activity in our life to remove the guilt.

If you have difficulty in considering God's forgiveness as a real act whereby your guilt is removed, you might be helped by writing down the specific sins of which God has made you aware. Use this list in your prayer of confession and mention each one specifically. Then find a friend whom you can trust and confess those same sins to him. This will help you recognize the reality of your confession. Next take the list of sins and destroy them. This will help you to realize that God has removed those sins from your life. You have brought them to Him and left them there. You no longer are to carry the haunting thoughts about them around with you.

Perhaps one of the most difficult aspects of forgiveness comes at the point of our willingness to forgive ourselves. Once we have confessed specific sins to God, have listed them on a sheet of paper, have shared them with a close friend, and have destroyed them, we must determine to forgive ourselves as completely as God has. We cannot afford the luxury of continuing to berate ourselves, downgrade ourselves, or punish ourselves for sins that have been forgiven by God.

Many people have great difficulty at this point. They continue to punish themselves for their wrongdoing. Myron Madden points out that such a process is in fact an attempt to reenact the atonement of Christ rather than accept it by faith. Since Christ died on the cross to pay the debt for our sins, it is useless for us to try to atone for our own sins by punishing ourselves. In fact, until we forgive ourselves, we have not actually accepted the forgiveness of God. As John Claypool puts it, it's like taking the garbage out to the street and then gathering it up and bringing it back into the house with us.[4] If we continue to carry about our own sins and the guilt for them, if we continue to blame ourselves and to punish ourselves, then it means we have not really left those sins in the hands of God. We have not accepted and lived. We gain help at this point by a deeper understanding of God's activity and forgiveness.

The divine involvement. We must not suppose that forgiveness comes easily for God, lest we are flippant about our sin. True holiness can never pass lightly over sin, and true love is always the most deeply involved. In Jesus' parable, the king who forgave his servant's debt had to be willing to lose the revenue involved. The prodigal's father had to be willing to live with the shame and hurt. The prodigal's elder brother, on the other hand, refused to forgive. He was not prepared to lose a calf, the place of the favored son, and the smirk of self-righteousness.

When we ask God to forgive sin, His righteousness requires that the wages of that sin be paid. God had to be willing to suffer in the place of everyone whose sin He forgives. This He did when Christ died, for "God was in Christ, reconciling the world unto himself" (II Cor. 5:19).

The psalmist saw the glory of God's forgiveness: "As far as the east is from the west, so far hath he removed our transgressions from us (Ps. 103:12). Yet Isaiah saw the price which God had to pay in order to send away our sins: "He was wounded for our transgressions, he was bruised for our iniquities: the chastisement of our peace was upon him; and with his stripes we are healed" (Isa. 53:5).

God looks on the forgiven person as a new person. The story is told about a minister traveling in Europe who was invited into a home for the night. The man of the house explained that his twelve-year-old boy had been adopted during the war years. The father told of the desperate condition in which they had found the boy, of his tattered clothing and worn-out shoes. The father explained that they gave the lad new clothing, but kept the old shoes as a reminder of how the boy looked when they found him. Periodically, the old shoes were brought out to remind the lad of his previous condition. The minister, noting that the boy looked hurt and ashamed while the father was speaking, thought to himself how glad he was that God doesn't continually drag out our old clothes.[5]

GRANTING FORGIVENESS

Jesus' parable about the unforgiving servant was not the first time He warned against an unforgiving spirit. In the Sermon on the Mount He said, "If ye forgive not men their trespasses, neither will your Father forgive your trespasses" (Matt. 6:15). We who so often say, "He doesn't deserve to be forgiven," need to realize that by its very nature, forgiveness is undeserved, else there would be nothing to forgive.

By sharing what you have received. Those who have received forgiveness are asked to share it, to pass it on. The God who established the grounds on which our sins are forgiven, who satisfied sin's wages in Christ's death, has thereby made the provision for the sins of those who wrong us. We are asked to forgive on the basis of Christ's death for sins. We are to let God's forgiveness flow through us to others.

I was once privileged to hear Corrie ten Boom, that

marvelous woman who risked her life to hide Jews during the German occupation in Holland. She told of the difficulty she had when confronted with the matter of forgiveness toward a German SS trooper.

Following a church service at which Miss ten Boom had spoken, a former SS guard came up to her smiling, expressed his appreciation for her message, shared with her that he had found Christ as Savior, and thrust forth his hand in friendship. Corrie remembered that he had once stood guard over her and her sister when they were being processed into the concentration camp at Ravensbruck.

She shared the feelings of enmity that swept over her as she remembered the mockery and the cruelty that man had shown toward her and her sister. The old, stored-up feelings of vengeance suddenly boiled through her. She tried to raise her hand to take his and found she could not do so. She was unable to feel the slightest spark of warmth or forgiveness.

With quivering voice, Corrie ten Boom told how she breathed a silent prayer asking for strength. She said to Christ, "I cannot forgive him. Give me Your forgiveness." Then suddenly there came a current of strength flowing through her arm and a sudden birth of love for this stranger swelled up in her heart. She was suddenly able not only to take this man's hand, but genuinely to forgive him. Then she shared with us her discovery—that the Christ who told us to love our enemies gives us, along with the command, the love itself with which to do it. The world's healing depends, not on our goodness nor our forgiveness, but upon His. We can let Christ's forgiveness flow through us to others.

We who pray "give us our daily bread" continue by saying, "and forgive us our debts as we forgive others."

The daily bread, and forgiveness, are both gifts. The latter is to be in proportion to our willingness to forgive.

It was Stephen's dying prayer of forgiveness toward his murderers that struck a note in the heart of Saul of Tarsus, the harsh persecutor of the early church (Acts 7:59–60). Seneca, the Stoic philosopher, once said that when a man injures you, you are to pay him back by a deed of kindness. He reasoned that it takes two to make a quarrel, and if one refuses to play the game, the quarrel will go out like a lamp without oil. Stephen refused to fight those who assaulted him, choosing rather to forgive them.

By identifying. Genuine forgiveness requires that you be willing to identify with the wrongdoer in such a way that you are willing to share the consequences of the wrong. The king in the parable was willing to enter into the debt and suffer loss. You must be willing to give up something you deserve in order to help the offender find life through another chance. In other words, to forgive is to stand alongside the wrong-doer, put yourself in his place, share his problem, as God in Christ stood in our place.

By forgetting. A part of God's forgiveness involves "remembering our sins no more." He forgets our sins! This does not involve a fault in memory, but a release of memory. To forget is to turn loose of, to cease to harbor and cherish. It is to purposely refuse to repeat some injury and continue to get mileage out of it. This can be accomplished only by God's help, and a determined effort to stand beside the offender in a healing way, to love him in the sense that you desire good for him rather than evil. The elder brother refused to forgive his prodigal brother because he didn't want to accept him, to will him good.

When we refuse to dwell on wrongs we have suffered, we are set free from the damaging and destructive practice of nursing grudges.

By allowing God to be judge. To forgive is to lay aside vengeance. God reminds us, "Vengeance is mine, I shall repay." Dorothy Sayers, in *Creed or Chaos*, speaks of the mischief-maker who would rather that evil be not cured than for it to be cured quietly and without violence. Such a person is not satisfied unless the offender is, as she says, "hounded down, beaten, and trampled on, and a savage war-dance executed upon the body." We are so prone to be judge, jury, and executioner, to suffer from grudgitis. Vengeance refuses to wait upon God, or to trust God: "Shall not the judge of all the earth do right?" (Gen. 18:25). Someone has observed that a fanatic is "one who does what God would do if He had all the facts."[6]

Ah, but you say, "How can I forgive him? He has not repented—he has not asked forgiveness!" We dare not excuse our spirit of vengeance on this ground. Admittedly, Jesus said, "If thy brother repent, forgive him" (Luke 17:3), but the Christian is to will good toward the offender whether he repents or not. The granting of forgiveness is for the offender's benefit and indeed his guilt remains until he asks forgiveness, but *the offer* of forgiveness by the extension of good will also benefits the one who offers. While I cannot release the offender from guilt, legally and morally, until he asks, I can personally forgive him without his asking.

This spirit of forgiveness is a necessity if we are to enjoy daily the forgiveness, and thus the peace, of God. We must understand why Jesus said we could only experience God's forgiveness by forgiving others. The reason is simple. The man who says, "I'll never forgive him," cannot himself be forgiven because he does not have the proper attitude necessary to approach God in penitence for his own sins.[7]

An unforgiving spirit shuts the door to the heart. God's forgiveness is shut out. When you let God's forgiveness in, your forgiveness can be let out. John Redhead, in *Learning to Have Faith*, uses the illustration of God's bucket of forgiving love and man's bucket of resentment toward a fellow man. Man must empty his bucket before he has any place to receive God's forgiveness.

When General Oglethorpe said, "I never forgive," John Wesley said, "Then I hope, sir, you never sin." Legend says that when Leonardo da Vinci painted the face of his enemy on Judas' shoulders, he was not then able to paint the face of Christ. But after he forgave his enemy and painted over the insult, he saw in a dream that very night the face of Christ.[8]

Robert Louis Stevenson, who always led his family in a daily devotional and the Lord's Prayer, stopped one day in the midst of the prayer and left the room. His wife, fearing he was ill, followed him. His explanation was that as he prepared to repeat "forgive us our debts as we forgive our debtors," he realized he was not fit that day to pray that prayer.

We cannot live without forgiveness—without receiving it or without granting it. The unforgiving mind becomes a sick mind, and before long this leads to a sick body. Often there is more harm done by the unforgiving spirit than was done by the sin one refuses to forgive. Hence, Jesus said there must be no limit to our forgiveness. The rabbis advocated forgiving a man three times, Peter suggested seven, but Jesus said seventy times seven. It is not a matter of mathematics, but of compassion.

Christ intended His church to be a fellowship of forgiveness. If there is a rift there, the infection of sin will find it, and ruin will follow. Only the forgiven and the forgiving can preach a gospel of forgiveness and offer real fellowship.

Jesus did not deal in theory. He forgave in the midst of real life and real blood. On the cross He cried, "Father, forgive them!" His Spirit enabled Stephen to do the same, and Paul, and thousands of others.

We know that we cannot live without forgiveness. Why do we keep trying?

Without forgiveness from God we shall live forever in hell; unless we grant forgiveness to others, we shall make a hell for ourselves on earth. We are not equipped to deal with stored up grudges. The resulting bitterness will destroy us. We must turn loose all ill feelings and be free of them, for happiness is impossible for anyone who refuses to forgive.

NOTES

1. Karl Meninger, *Whatever Became of Sin?* (New York: Hawthorne Books, Inc., 1973), p. 188.

2. *Look Magazine,* February 2, 1960.

3. Jay Adams, *Competent to Counsel* (Grand Rapids: Baker Book House, 1970), pp. 103–104.

4. John Claypool, "Forgiveness As Event" (unpublished sermon).

5. Jefferson Kesterson, "Let the Past Be Past," *Pulpit Digest* 50 (December, 1970): 36.

6. Ernest T. Campbell, "Jesus on Vengeance," *Pulpit Digest* 50 (June, 1970): 26.

7. *The Interpreter's Bible,* George Buttrick, ed. (New York: Abingdon Press, 1957) VII: 314.

8. Ibid.

For as the body
without the spirit is dead,
so faith without works
is dead also.
(James 2:26)

6
Take Some Risks

■Have you ever begun a letter, written for a while, then crumpled it in your fist, muttering, "That's not what I want to say," and reached for a new sheet of paper? Have you ever felt that way about life? Do you grow tired of the well-worn ruts that monotonously guide your activities day in and day out? Have you ever yearned with Omar Khayyam to "smash this sorry scheme of things entire and mold it nearer to your heart's desire?"

Our Lord said, "I am come that they might have life, and that they might have it more abundantly" (John 10:10). But no real change can enter your life apart from your willingness to take some risks. You can't lock life in a box and expect anything to come from it. The first day of school for a five year old is an ordeal, a risk. But growth requires that risks be taken. A new job is a risk. Marriage is a risk. Any time you open yourself in love to others, you take a chance on being hurt. But the alternative is stagnation, emptiness, and cynicism. To remove all risk from life, is to remove life itself. In Victor Hugo's *Les Miserables*, Jean Valjean lies on his deathbed and looks up at his adopted daughter, for whom he has sacrificed all things, and because of whom he is dying, and says, "It is nothing to die; it is frightful not to live."[1] Much of our unhappiness comes from the gnawing feeling that life is passing us by, that we are never really going to live.

Sooner or later, each of us must realize that success or failure is something we must assume responsibility for. In an effort to emphasize this, Jesus once told a parable about three men and what they did with their opportunities. The master of an estate, before taking a journey, called in his three servants and divided among them a considerable amount of resources. One servant was given five talents, another two talents, and another one talent. The first two men invested the talents given them and, upon the master's return, were able to report the profit that had been made. However, the third man, fearing failure, dug a hole in the earth, buried it, then retrieved it upon the master's return. The first two men who had invested what had been given them were commended. The third was severely reprimanded for his failure. The one talent that had been given to him was taken away from him and given to the first servant who had taken the risk and put his talents to work. The poor man who had buried his talent, and therefore lost it, was called an "unprofitable servant" (Matt. 25:14–30).

The major point of this parable is the man who failed. He probably had a touching story about hard luck, adverse circumstances, and the fact that while others were given many talents, he was given only one. Yet, Jesus did not look on the man as one who had been mistreated. This man was accountable for his failure. The final evaluation of his failure was rather abrupt: "Take therefore the talent from him. . . . and cast ye the unprofitable servant into outer darkness: there shall be weeping and gnashing of teeth" (Matt. 25:28,30).

Jesus was not giving a short course on financial ventures in this parable; He was talking about investing life. What one does with what one has will determine whether he ultimately succeeds or fails. We need to look more closely at how the man in the parable failed so that we won't follow in his footsteps.

THE FORMULA FOR FAILURE

Although everyone wants to succeed in life, it is amazing how many follow the formula for failure found in this passage of Scripture.

Plan for failure. The man in the parable planned to fail. He was so fearful of failing that he made certain he would by attempting nothing. He took what he had—the one talent—and buried it. He chose to live by fear and not by faith. Fear is the poorest of all motivations, for it paralyzes our strengths.

Robert Schuller has written what he calls the "Possibility Thinkers' Creed."

> When faced with a mountain
> I will not quit.
> I will keep on striving
> Until I

> Climb over,
>   Find a pass through,
> Tunnel underneath,
>   Or simply stay and
> Turn the mountain
>   Into a gold mine!
> With God's help![2]

E. Stanley Jones tells about an army chaplain whose testimony was that his life was transformed once he discovered the philosophy of George Washington Carver: "Take what you have and make something out of it." Carver took what the South had—clay, sweet potatoes, and peanuts. Out of clay he made paints; out of sweet potatoes he made one hundred fifty commercial products; and out of peanuts he made three hundred commercial products. Once when Jones met Carver he said to him, "Dr. Carver, you and I are in the same great business. You are discovering wonders in peanuts, and I am discovering wonders in people, both of them wrapped in strange wrappings."[3]

Develop a life pattern of failure. That the servant buried his whole potential would lead one to suspect that this was merely part of a pattern he had developed. Failure produces failure. For many people patterns develop early in life. Take, for instance, a student in school who decides that spending time with his books is not worth it. As a result he is reprimanded. No longer respecting himself, he tends to identify with the losers. He drifts into the wrong crowd and lives up to his pattern of failure. From being an outcast in the classroom he becomes an outcast in society. Before long he begins to bury himself and his potential in drugs, sex, and basic forms of dishonesty.

Blame others. From the moment the useless servant

decided to bury his potential, he began planning excuses. In fact, explaining his failure was more important to him than avoiding failure. He blamed the master (who in the parable represents God), by saying that he was a hard man, reaping where he had not sown, and gathering where he had not strawed. But Jesus said that the man's excuses would not be accepted.

THE SECRET OF SUCCESS

The other two servants in the parable decided to spend their time working rather than laying a groundwork of excuses. They invested their lives in behalf of their master. That each of them was given more talents than the useless servant is beside the point. The key is that they used what they had. We don't have equal abilities, but we can put forth an equal effort.

There is no final failure for anyone who invests himself in the service of the Lord. "Therefore my beloved brethren, be ye stedfast, unmoveable, always abounding in the work of the Lord, forasmuch as ye know that your labour is never in vain in the Lord" (I Cor. 15:58), is God's promise.

On a recent Merv Griffin show, four millionaires, each under the age of forty, were interviewed. The last of the four was in his early thirties and was worth eighteen million dollars. When he was asked, "Is that enough money?" he replied, "If you mean, is it enough to live on, the answer is yes. But if you mean, do I plan to stop at this point, the answer is no. My objective is to make fifty million dollars." He went on to explain that it was not that he needed the money, but making money was the business he was in, and money is the way you keep score, like in a game of Monopoly. At that point, Griffin said, "I'm sure then that you are happy."

"Yes," the millionaire replied, "but not because of my wealth. I have many friends who are wealthy and not one of them is happy. On the other hand, I have a gardener and a maid, both of whom have little money, and both of whom are very happy." He said that he saw no direct relationship between money and happiness.

Then the young millionaire was asked what it took to make a person happy. This was his answer: "Something to do; someone to love; and something to look forward to."

Looking back at the useless servant, we see that he had chosen to have nothing to do. We do not know whether or not he had someone to love, but we do know he had very little to look forward to. We learn from the lives of the other two servants that the person who invests himself for the master gets the reward of hearing, "Well done," and of being given more work to do.

WHEN FAILURES COME

Anyone who dares to find life will have his share of failures. Do not suppose that a few failures along the way can keep you from the life you desire to have. Some of the deepest lessons of life are learned from our failures, and out of them often come the greatest opportunities for new direction in life. Sometimes a failure is God's way of telling us to take a new turn.

Thomas Edison lost two million dollars worth of equipment and records along with much of his life's work in a fire in 1914 that nearly destroyed the great Edison Industries in West Orange, New Jersey. His son, Charles, found him near the fire, his face ruddy in the glow, his white hair blown by winter winds. Edison told his son to find his mother and bring her to him, saying, "She'll never see anything like this again as long as she lives."

Next morning, walking about the charred embers of so many of his hopes and dreams, the sixty-seven-year-old Edison said, "There is great value in disaster. All our mistakes are burned up. Thank God we can start anew."[4]

One of Germany's leading psychiatrists operates a clinic for alcoholics and neurotics in the Black Forest. He gave an interesting insight on the fact that the patients and the families who cannot pay have their bill paid by the government. He said that today in Germany no one is allowed to fail. Looking at history, he said that one hundred years ago families sent their failures, their black sheep members, to America. There, they had to make good or die. He further commented that America had become great through those same black sheep. It was they who had built America, and had, in the process, found themselves. His commentary was that where men are not allowed to fail, they never have the chance to find themselves.[5]

If we, in an effort to avoid all risks, bury our potential, we will gradually lose even that which we have. Life, bit by bit, will lose all meaning, joy, excitement, and hope. When one arrives at this point he has indeed become a "useless servant." Charlotte Brontë has well said, "Better to try all things and find all empty, than to try nothing and leave your life a blank."[6]

We should not fear failures, but we must merely determine not to let them become permanent. We must decide to learn from them rather than be paralyzed by them. I heard a corporation executive say that the company he once worked with refused to hire men in leadership positions who had not known at least one significant failure. They wanted someone who had been through failure and survived, who had learned to try again. They did not want someone in a place of leadership who had never been tested by the fires of failure. Temporary failures are a part of our growth. They may become the foundation on which we at last discover life.

A CAUTION ABOUT PERSPECTIVE

Winning and losing, succeeding and failing, can be illusions. Jesus warned that it was possible for a person to think he was succeeding only to discover at the end of life that he had failed. For this reason He warned, "What shall it profit a man, if he gain the whole world, and lose his own soul?" (Mark 8:36).

Those who please God are those who have, in His name, invested their lives in His kingdom, in works of compassion, in acts of kindness, in ministries of witness. To live by faith is to dare to invest yourself in the lives of others, and in His church, in the name of Christ.

Authentic faith calls us to a life of risk and investment. Karl Wallenda and his family are without doubt the greatest high-wire acrobats in the world. In 1972 a tragedy occurred. Several members of the Wallenda troupe fell from the wire and were killed while performing in Detroit. To the surprise of everyone, a few days later those who survived were back on the high wire repeating their famous act. When questioned by a reporter, Karl

Wallenda explained their decision to go on. He said, "To be on the wire is life. All else is waiting." In the spiritual realm, to live by faith is to invest yourself in the name of the Father. To do otherwise, is to suffer an illusion of success.

A DECISION ABOUT GOD

One's ultimate success or failure depends on how seriously he takes God. No one is a success without God. The two faithful servants were told that now they could "enter into the joy of the Lord." The heavenly Father has a goal for each of us. He wants us to discover life with all the fullness He intended. Yet there is a risk involved: We must dare to give Christ the central place in our lives. When our Lord talked about the possibilities of coming alive spiritually, He did so in terms of the simple patching of a garment. He said: "No man putteth a piece of new cloth unto an old garment, for that which is put in to fill up taketh from the garment, and the rent is made worse" (Matt. 9:16). Most apparel in those days was woolen, and would shrink when first washed. Therefore, to use a new piece of cloth that had not yet been shrunken to patch an old garment would result in the new piece shrinking, thus tearing a larger hole in the old cloth.

Jesus was warning against the easy way of adding Him to life. Just as putting a new patch on an old garment accomplishes nothing, so Jesus is warning that to try to add Him to one's old life is meaningless. One of the problems faced by missionaries in India is that the Hindu already has one hundred or more saviors. To add Christ as another savior on his long list is meaningless. This problem is not confined to India. All too often this has been the basic American approach. We are willing to add Christ to our list of ingredients that make up life. We are willing to add the church to our list of organizations to which we belong. In this approach to Christ, man remains in control as lord of all. The old garment is still the old garment.

All areas of life find meaning only as they properly relate to Christ. When He becomes Lord of our lives, we must practice what is spoken of in economics as zero budgeting. Government leaders insist that every government agency justify its importance and its budget each year, or perish. This same kind of agenda needs to be followed by every Christian. Every ingredient of life that cannot properly relate to the lordship of Christ should be deleted.

Cecil Samara, the super-fan of Oklahoma University, has gone all the way in something he believes in. He actually has "Big Red" permanently enameled in red on his front teeth. His testimony is, "I have lived for O.U., and I want to die that way. I've got a red and white casket already bought and paid for. I'm to be buried with my finger pointing up to say that Oklahoma is number one. The music will be 'Boomer Sooner'!"

Most of us would feel Cecil Samara is a little extreme. But it is refreshing to hear of one, even if he seems to be a little crazy, who is firmly committed to something. Most of us have not begun to give Christ the place in our life that Cecil Samara has given football in his.

Arnold Toynbee devoted his life to the study of history. Toward the end of his years, he gave us an overview of the various "saviors" of the world:

When we set out on this quest we found ourselves moving in the midst of a mighty host, but, as we have pressed forward, the marchers, company by company have fallen out of the race. The first to fail were the swordsmen, the next the archaists, and futurists, the next the philosophers, until only gods were left in the running. At the final ordeal of death, few, even of those would-be saviour gods have dared to put their title to the test by plunging into the icy river. And now, as we stand and gaze with our eyes fixed upon the farther shore, a single figure rises from the flood and straightway fills the whole horizon. There is the Saviour; 'and the pleasure of the Lord shall prosper in his hand; he shall see of the travail of his soul and shall be satisfied.'[7]

We never come alive spiritually, nor do we experience spiritual growth until we have given Christ the proper place in life. Perhaps it boils down to the words of Myron Madden in his haunting question: "How many people do you allow behind the altar of your soul?" Madden explains that there is actually room in that "holy of holies" behind the altar of your soul for two people—you and God. If someone else has taken God's place, and you are more interested in pleasing them than pleasing God, you are in trouble. On the other hand, if you have relinquished your place so that someone else is telling you what God wants you to do with your life, then you have merely become that other person's shadow.

Jesus went on to make another very meaningful statement: "Neither do men put new wine into old bottles (wineskins); else the bottles (wineskins) break, and the wine runneth out, and the bottles (wineskins) perish: but they put new wine into new bottles (new wineskins), and both are preserved" (Matt. 9:17). Although the King

James Version chose to translate the Greek word "wineskins" as "bottles" to be more up-to-date, we lose the full meaning involved unless we recognize that Jesus was speaking of containers made from the hide of goats. When the new hide was made into a container for wine, it was still pliable. However, as the wineskins grew older, they became hardened and set, and wine would inevitably split the containers.

Jesus is saying that life must be open to His direction, to His change. If life becomes hard and set, poured into a mold, there is no room for God's direction in life. Spiritual growth requires that you remain open to deeper levels of relationship with the Living God. Christ never told anyone, "You're great just as you are." Rather, He in effect said to each person, "I accept you as you are—but there is much growing for you, much newness ahead. You need a whole reorienting of life's purposes."

Jonathan Livingston Seagull has in it a great truth. Other seagulls looked on flying as a means of getting something to eat, but Jonathan Seagull thought one should eat only in order to fly—not fly in order to eat. Most of us are like the other seagulls. We live in order to work for the goods of this world. Christ would have us take a deeper look to see that we are made primarily for living. We should not live merely in order to eat; we should eat in order to live.

NOTES

1. Victor, Hugo, *Les Miserables* (New York: Random House, Inc., n.d.), p. 1218.

2. Robert H. Schuller, *You Can Become the Person You Want to Be* (New York: Hawthorne Books, Inc., 1973), p. 28.

3. E. Stanley Jones, *The Christ of the American Road* (New York: Abingdon-Cokesbury Press, 1944), pp. 239–40.

4. Norman Vincent Peale, "The Amazing Power of Positive Thinking," *Proclaim* 6 (January-March, 1976): 34.

5. Bruce Larson, *The Relational Revolution* (Waco, TX: Word Books, 1976), p. 137.

6. Charlotte Brontë, *Shirley* (New York: E. P. Dutton and Company, 1940), p. 399.

7. Arnold J. Toynbee, *A Study of History* (Oxford: Oxford University Press, 1947), p. 547.

My sheep hear my voice,
and I know them,
and they follow me.
(John 10:27)

7

Discover the
Will of God

■There are dozens of kinds of lives we could choose to live, but we will find real life—life uninterrupted even by death—only when we join our lives with the power of God and find direction within His will.

Jesus said to His disciples, "If any man will come after me, let him deny himself, and take up his cross, and follow me" (Matt. 16:24). He was not only telling them that He was to die on a cross, but that they too must carry crosses if they were to follow. The *cross* is God's will for our lives. For Christ to do the will of the Father meant He must die. We must be willing to do whatever God wants us to do at all times.

Many are afraid of the will of God. They have the haunting idea that God will lead them into oblivion and uselessness, into unhappiness and emptiness. They fear that God, like humans or computers, may make some horrible mistake.

God makes no mistakes when He draws the blueprint for our lives. God's will has to do with two basic areas: 1) the kind of person you become, and 2) the way you spend the person you become.

If we are to truly find life we must begin a journey marked off by God. Thoreau said, "Read not the times; read the eternities." One must step to the tune of a different drummer, listen to the divine music that bids him follow. The beaten path is seldom the will of God. We can learn much from the words of an anonymous author:

> One day, through the primieval wood
> A calf walked home, as good calves should;
> But made a trail all bent askew
> A crooked trail, as all calves do.
>
> That trail was taken up next day
> By a dog that passed that way;
> And then a wise bellwether sheep
> Pursued the trail o'er vale and steep;
> And drew the flock behind him, too,
> As all good bellwethers always do.
>
> And from that day, o'er hill and glade
> Through those old woods the path was made;
> And many *men* wound in and out
> And dodged, and turned, and bent about
> And uttered words of righteous wrath
> Because 'twas such a crooked path.
> But still they followed. . . . do not laugh . . .
> The first migrations of that calf.
>
> The years passed on in swiftness fleet,
> The road became a village street
> And this, before men were aware
> A city's crowded thoroughfare.

Each day a hundred thousand rout
  Trailed that zig-zag calf about
And o'er his crooked journey went
  The traffic of a continent.
A hundred thousand men were led
  By one calf near two centuries dead.

A moral lesson this might teach
  Were I ordained and called to preach
For *men* are prone to go it blind
  Along the calf-paths of the mind;
They work away from sun to sun
  To do what *other* men have done;
They follow in the beaten track
  And out and in and forth and back
And still their devious course pursue
  To keep the path that others do.

But how the wise old wood-gods laugh
  Who saw that first primieval calf![1]

However, do not presume that God's will goes in a straight line just because it seldom travels the beaten path. When God led the Israelites from Egyptian bondage Scripture records: "God led them not out through the way of the land of the Philistines, although that was nearer... but God led the people about, through the way of the wilderness..." (Exod. 13:17—18). The journey from Egypt to Canaan was but two hundred miles, a ten-day journey by camel caravan, but God led the Israelites for forty years in the wilderness before they arrived to possess the land. God took the wandering route because the people were not yet ready to enter the Promised Land. Their faith was too weary (Heb. 4:6). God seldom allows us to enter "promised lands" too quickly because "too much too soon" is the formula for mediocrity.[2]

THE COST IS GREAT

Christ admitted that the cost of finding life is tremendous. He said, "If any man will come after me, let him *deny himself* . . . and *lose his life*." Here Jesus is using two approaches to explain how one is able to discover God's will. To deny oneself is to give up the idea that "this is my life to do with as I please." This is also what Christ meant by, "Whosoever will *lose his life* for my sake shall find it."

Trading our wills for His will might mean not only giving up our own claims to our lives, but the claims our parents or other family members might make as well. The poet catches this in a very poignant way:

I said let me walk in the fields,
    Christ said go walk in the town.
I said 'There are no flowers there.'
    He said no flowers, but a crown.
I said, 'But I shall miss the light, and my friends will miss
       me they say.'
    He said, 'Choose tonight, if I am to miss you or they.'
I pleaded for time to be given,
    He said is it hard to decide?
It will not seem hard in Heaven to have followed the steps
       of your guide.
So I took one look at the fields,
    Then set my face for the town.
He said 'My child, do you yield?
    Do you trade the flowers for the crown?'
Then into His hand went mine,
    And into my heart came He.
And I walk with a light divine,
    The path that I feared to see.[3]

THE REWARDS ARE GREAT

Although the costs for finding God's will are great, the rewards are even greater. Jesus used words like *profit* and *gain* to highlight this fact. "For what is a man profited, if he shall gain the whole world, and lose his own soul? or what shall a man give in exchange for his soul?" (Matt. 16:26). The soul is one's total being, not some tiny spark deep within. It concerns all of this earthly life and all of life beyond the grave.

Babies demand each need be fulfilled the moment it is recognized, but maturity comes when a person is willing to postpone fulfillment, to deny the present that the future may have a chance. I recently heard the new United States figure skating champion say in an interview that she knew practically no other sixteen-year-olds because of the discipline she had to follow day by day in practice. Headed for the Olympics, she was willing to deny herself for the moment that she might reach the realization of a dream. Self-denial for the sake of Christ is for those who want a real identity.

Count von Zinzendorf became a leader of the Moravian brethren and their tremendous missionary movement of the eighteenth century. He turned his back on earthly honors and high position to give his life to the spreading of the Gospel. One day when the young count was burning some old documents and scraps of parchment, one piece escaped the flames. He threw it back into the fire, but it obstinately refused to burn. He idly picked it up and read, "Oh, let us in thy nail-prints see, our calling and election free." He was suddenly aware that God was speaking to him through the words on this scrap of paper, challenging him to follow Christ. Zinzendorf's motto became, "I have one passion; it is He and He alone." Once you become aware of the will of God in your life, it becomes a scrap of paper that won't burn. It has your name on it, and Christ's name on it, and you become aware that the Holy Spirit has joined these names together.[4]

To turn one's back on the will of God is, at best, to seek after and accumulate only that which is temporary, to approach God knowing you have lived as an untrusting, rebellious child.

At worst, to reject God's will is to approach the end of life with nothing beyond but hell. One must live with the knowledge that everyone who followed his steps was deceived, that those he cared for the most were the most harmed.

HOW TO BEGIN THE SEARCH

Although there is no simple formula by which one can discover the will of God, there are some very practical steps one can take.

Thank God that you are you. Look into the mirror and accept your appearance, age, education, health, financial status, and limitations. Then genuinely thank God for who you are.

Stop worrying about failure. God does not call us to be successful, but to be faithful. Most people never try anything because they are afraid of failure. This guarantees failure, for the greatest failure is never to try.

Begin doing what you already know is the will of

God. There are some things that God wills for everyone. First, He wills that everyone be saved (I Tim. 2:3–4).

God also wills that everyone *belong* to the church. He warns against "forsaking the assembling of yourselves together" (Heb. 10:25). Belonging to the church is more than attending church or having one's name on the church roll. It is being an active part of the church—a steward. God has chosen the church as the instrument for carrying out His purposes on earth.

Communicate with God daily. Have prayer and devotional reading of the Scriptures daily and you will discover that the Bible is God's letter addressed especially to you.

Make a list of your present schedule of activities and personal habits. The will of God has to do with the kind of person you are becoming, and the way you are spending that person. Ask of every item on your list, "Is this my will? Is this God's will? Is this both my will and God's will?" Then begin an elimination.

Talk with other Christians. God often will use other Christians to help us discover our usefulness. Others may be aware of opportunities for service that we have overlooked. Stay open to any offered opportunity. This does not mean you must do everything that someone asks you to do. It merely means you must remain sensitive to God's leadership.

Be open to inner impressions. You can never be sure just how God will reveal His will to you. It may come through your discovery of someone who is hurting, and your awareness that you ought to help that hurt. God may use small incidents to begin the first faltering steps that will lead at last to His will.

Make yourself and your resources available to

God. Life is found in "giving it away" in His name. What God originates, He will empower. Never rule out the impossible merely because it seems impossible. God doesn't just develop your potential; He gives you a whole new potential. Paul said, "I beseech you therefore, brethren, by the mercies of God, that you present your bodies a living sacrifice, holy, acceptable unto God, which is your reasonable service" (Rom. 12:1). God blesses everything we offer to Him, and day by day God will give us a larger picture. Though at the outset, discovering the will of God may seem to be a very difficult thing, the real difficulty does not lie at that point. The real difficulty comes once His will is ascertained, and we realize we must follow. One must be ready to give all before he begins a serious search for God's will. We are not left to ourselves to find His will; our major step is to report to God for duty.

THE DECISION IS YOURS

God never forces anyone to follow Him. Christ said, "*If* any man will come after me. . . ." This means we must face squarely our own cross (God's will for our lives). When Christ told His disciples that He was to die on the cross, Simon Peter tried to convince Him that this would be the wrong choice. Jesus told Simon that in those words He heard the voice of Satan. If you take seriously God's will, you, too, will hear the voice of Satan. It may come from the words of family members or friends—someone will try to convince you that God's will costs too much. However, this is a decision you, and you alone must make.

When Jesus asked, "What shall a man give in exchange for his soul?" He was in effect saying, "There is no exchange possible with God." You either give Him all your life, or you give Him nothing. Do not suppose that by giving God your time, you have given Him your life. He has that only if you give Him your will.

Robert Frost stood at a fork in the road, undecided which path to take. When he finally chose, he did it with the recognition of what was involved in his choice. He did it knowing he was beginning a journey to a final destiny. He made the choice knowing he would never again stand at that fork in the road. He then concluded:

> I shall be telling this with a sigh
>   Somewhere ages and ages hence:
> Two roads diverged in a wood, and I—
>   I took the one less travelled by,
> And that has made all the difference.

Do you want to find life? It is a choice of God's will that makes all the difference. It's up to you. But we have to be willing to grow. We have to believe that God is capable of molding our lives. We must turn loose and follow Him. He looks down the years ahead and knows what we can be. We have to dare to believe that He can truly transform any life—even our own.

We tend to live up to what people think of us. We must grasp the importance of living up to what God thinks of us. In the words of Robert Schuller, "I am not what I think I am; I am not what you think I am; I am what I think, you think, I am." God believes we are somebody. He calls us His sons and daughters. Growth is determining to live up to His expectations. To discover God's will is to discover that God thinks we are capable of a great deal. Daring to act upon that premise, we will be transformed!

NOTES

1. "The Calf Path," author unknown, in Ralph W. Nabor, Jr., and Cal Thomas, *Target Group Evangelism* (Nashville: Broadman Press, 1975), pp. 127–28.

2. J. Wallace Hamilton, *Serendipity* (Old Tappan, NJ: Fleming H. Revell Co., 1967), p. 155.

3. Poem by George McDonald.

4. James Stewart, "What Lack I Yet?" *Pulpit Digest* 55 (May-June, 1975): 9.

Jesus saith to him,
I am the way, the truth,
and the life.
(John 14:6)

8

Live the Truth

■We must love the truth (I John 3:18), and walk in the truth (II John 4). The reason for discovering the will of God is that we may discover the truth as it relates to our own lives. Jesus had this concept in mind when He said: "Ye shall know the truth, and the truth shall make you free" (John 8:32).

There have been times when I was afraid to know the truth and went to great extremes to deceive myself lest the truth break in. Before becoming a minister, I was a farmer and rancher for several years. I knew, from the depth of my soul, that God's truth for my life led in another direction, but I refused to face it. Only after several years of spiritual agony was I ready to face up to God's truth for my life and surrender to His call to the ministry. But preachers are not the only ones who have to struggle with the truth of what God would have one do with his life. Every Christian must go through that same struggle. Therefore it is important that you determine whether you really want to know God's whole truth for your life.

We are quite willing to pursue scientific truth to its ultimate because we are not threatened by it. But to delve into spiritual truth requires that we open our lives to whatever changes God might have for us. Truth involves accepting the fact that we have been made in the image of God, but that we have personally sinned and marred that image. Truth involves the recognition that in Jesus Christ we have been remade, redeemed, and called to care as He cared, love as He loved, be honest as He was honest, just as He was just, merciful as He was merciful. Truth requires that we be involved in life in the name of Jesus Christ.

Truth is a way of life based on the reality of two worlds. We live in a visible world made of material things, but at the same time we live in an invisible world, a spiritual world. Unless we acknowledge the unseen Christ and His unseen kingdom as the unifying truth that binds together all aspects of life, we shall live in disharmony.

Francis Schaeffer, in his book, *The God Who Is There*, uses the illustration of a symphony composed of musicians who are all playing their favorite songs at the same time. Two men standing outside the door discuss what is happening. The first man is exalted. "Isn't this wonderful," he said, "each man is playing his own song and doing what he likes to do." The second man listening at the door sadly notes that none of the musicians has tuned his instrument and that there is nothing but bedlam going on since they cannot agree to play one song together. All persons who leave the truth of Jesus Christ out of their lives, supposing they are finding themselves by doing their own thing, will experience the same disharmony.

DARING TO DO RIGHT

In late June of 1972 an airplane was skyjacked. The villain demanded over five hundred thousand dollars in cash, then bailed out near Peru, Indiana. Although law enforcement officers combed the area looking for the skyjacker and the money, they found neither. From other clues they were able to trace the man to his home where he was taken into custody. A farmer just outside of Peru, Indiana, found the ransom money and called the authorities as any honest man would do. Out of appreciation, the airline offered him a ten thousand dollar reward and sent along a photographer to take a picture of him accepting it. To their amazement, the farmer refused the reward, not because he did not want a reward, but because he said ten thousand dollars was not enough for his honesty since the skyjacker had nearly gotten away with half a million dollars.

A rich young businessman once came to Jesus indicating a desire to be His disciple. Jesus looked at the promising young man and saw in his heart the god of money. Jesus then demanded that the young man dispose of all his possessions if he was serious about following Him. On the heels of this experience, Peter looked at Christ and asked, "We have forsaken all, and followed thee; what shall we have therefore?" (Matt. 19:27). In effect he was asking, "Does it pay to do right?" Probably everyone has, in some moment of doubt or weakness, asked himself the same question. Does it pay to be honest? Does it pay to serve God? Does it pay to work in the church? Does it pay to tithe? Does it pay to live by a godly moral code? Daring to do right is made easier if we examine the alternatives.

CONSEQUENCES OF DOING WRONG

Later in his life Peter called the consequences of wrongdoing the "reward of unrighteousness" (II Peter 2:13). This reward comes from allowing immediate benefits to become the basis for all decisions. Let's look again at the farmer. If he had kept the money, he would have had a type of reward in that he had a small fortune laid aside for his private use. Yet every time he saw a car drive up to his house he would have wondered if it was the police. Every time he heard a siren he would have wondered if police had discovered him and were coming to arrest him. Every time he left home he would be afraid that someone would discover his hidden fortune. He could not have spent it, at least for years, without being discovered. He would have been like the man who swallowed the egg and was afraid to move for fear it would break, and afraid to sit still for fear it would hatch.

To have kept the money would have cost what every act of wrong costs—the loss of personal integrity. The word *integrity* is closely allied with the word *integer*, a term used to describe a whole number, when speaking of arithmetic. The root meaning in each case is that of wholeness. An integer is a whole number. Integrity is that quality which marks a whole person.

If wrong doing becomes a way of life, sensitivity will be

destroyed in the soul, capacity for deep and lasting feelings will be smothered, and self-respect will be annihilated. One of the leading psychiatrists at Texas Christian University said recently that guilt produces a kind of short circuit in the mental processes that keeps a person from being able to concentrate on other things and carry on other meaningful activities. The reality of guilt is attested by the fact that so many people who have escaped police detection later turn themselves in. There comes a time when men have to talk to someone else about their sins because they can no longer live with guilt haunting them every moment. Often physical maladies such as heart attacks, ulcers, and high blood pressure are the result of living lies instead of the truth.

Some men are able to ignore their consciences until they are on their deathbeds. The most famous story concerning this awesome experience is of Faust who sold his soul to the devil as a young man in order to have fame and fortune. But as life came to its end and Satan prepared to claim his prize, Faust found he had a "reward" that he did not want to die with.

THE REWARD OF DOING RIGHT

Peter, on learning that the rich businessman that came to Christ would not be allowed to enter heaven, asked Christ what the disciples could expect as a reward. He answered: "Ye which have followed me, in the regeneration when the Son of man shall sit in the throne of his glory, ye also shall sit upon twelve thrones, judging the twelve tribes of Israel. And every one that hath forsaken houses, or brethren, or sisters, or father, or mother, or wife, or children, or lands, for my name's sake, shall receive an hundredfold, and shall inherit everlasting life" (Matt. 19:28–29). The reward—a spiritual reward that never perishes—will come in eternity, after Christ has judged the nations.

Jesus explained to Simon Peter that the reward of doing right does not come immediately, and should not be expected in this life. Although we do have a good feeling about doing right, we would like for God to be a little more discriminating in the way He passes out earthly blessings. He sends rain on the just, and on the unjust, and causes His sun to shine on the evil, and on the good. With Peter, we would like to ask what our reward will be.

To understand the reward that comes from doing right, we need to look at Abraham, the man of faith. When Abraham was no longer able to stay with his nephew Lot because their servants were constantly bickering, he gave Lot the choice of either the mountain or the valley. Lot, being a wise businessman, choose the well-watered valley and so moved to Sodom.

Abraham had done what was right, yet had gotten only the barren mountainside. Shortly thereafter several rampaging kings swept down upon the twin cities of Sodom and Gomorrah and plundered them, taking not only the wealth therein, but also Abraham's nephew, Lot. Abraham gathered his own kindred and servants together and pursued the villains, overtaking and subduing them. On his return to Sodom, Abraham gave back all the riches that had been taken from the king of Sodom and from the city. The king of Sodom was so grateful that he offered to give the recovered riches as a reward. Abraham, being wise enough to know that one has a tendency to get tied up with those who bestow lavish rewards, said: "I will not take from a thread even to a shoelatchet, and that I will not take any thing that is thine, lest thou shouldest say, 'I have made Abram rich'" (Gen. 14:23).

Once again, Abraham had done what was right, yet received nothing for it. In the aftermath of these two experiences, God addressed Abraham: "Fear not, Abraham: I am thy shield, and thy exceeding great reward" (Gen. 15:1). To have God as our reward means we will have the joy of integrity before God, and the peaceful assurance that only He can give about the present and the future.

Speaking of His return, our Lord said: "And, behold, I come quickly; and my reward is with me, to give every man according as his work shall be" (Rev. 22:12). In a sense, our greatest reward will be Christ Himself.

THE OPTION: SON OR SLAVE?

To refuse to live the truth is to become "the slave of sin" (John 8:34). But to place God on the thrones of our hearts is to become "sons of God" (I John 3:2). This same commitment by which we become His sons in faith, is a commitment to what is right, for God is holy and His children are to be holy.

Doing the truth involves knowing when to say yes and when to say no. William James once said:

> Not that I would not, if I could, be both handsome and fat and well-dressed, and a great athlete, and make a million a year, be a wit, a bon vivant, and a lady-killer as well as a philosopher; a philanthropist, statesman, warrior, an African explorer as well as a 'tone-poet' and saint, but the

thing is simply impossible. The millionaire's work would run counter to the saint's; the bon vivant and the philosopher would trip each other up; the philosopher and the lady-killer could not well keep house in the same tenement of clay. . . . So the secret of his truest, strongest, deepest self must review the list carefully and pick out the one on which he can stake his salvation.[1]

We must look above the promises of reward and see that the real option is that we become a son of God or a slave of the world and our sins. In 1845 the United States perpetrated a war against Mexico on the flimsy doctrine of manifest destiny—the belief that this country should stretch from one ocean to the other even though there were some Mexicans who owned some land in between. President Polk levied a special tax to make manifest destiny possible. Henry David Thoreau refused to pay the tax and was put in jail. Ralph Waldo Emerson went to see him and said, "Henry, Henry, why are you here?" Thoreau replied, "Mr. Emerson, why aren't you here?" We look at the cross, and like the disciples, we ask why Christ had to die there. Yet if we look closely, we will find Christ asking us why we are not also living the way of the cross.

I am convinced that Judas did not betray Christ for a mere thirty pieces of silver. He saw a pattern developing in the life of Christ and realized there was "nothing in it for him." He had seen the miraculous power of Christ and somehow felt that if certain incidents could be triggered this power would be brought to play and an overthrow of Rome would result. If this happened, there would be something in it for him. Judas thought that by his betrayal he could bring a confrontation that would result in Christ's triumph as Messiah. Somehow Judas had always been able to resist real sonship. He had always kept prominent in his life that which would benefit him instead of that which was right. Decision by decision, each brick of his personal prison was cemented together until at last the only escape possible for him was to take his own life.

Only those who live the truth can have any sense of assurance about their destination. John G. Williams says:

> Anybody who finds himself (however unwillingly) embarked on the journey of life without at some point satisfying himself about the aim of the journey and where it is ultimately intended to lead is in something of the same situation as a man might be if he were to set out from New York in a leaking rowboat, without any oars or provisions, chart or compass, and hope to make a successful voyage to nowhere-in-particular! He may of course, for what seems good reason, be quite convinced that there is no purpose and no destination; then he can only hope to ride out the storms and enjoy what good weather there is and resign himself to sinking gracefully when the end comes.[2]

FORMULA FOR LIVING THE TRUTH

Give each day to God. Romans 12:1–2 provides some simple guidelines which, if followed, will start us on our journey of living the truth. "I beseech you therefore, brethren, by the mercies of God, that ye present your bodies a living sacrifice, holy, acceptable unto God, which is your reasonable service. And be not conformed to this world: but be transformed by the renewing of your mind, that you may prove what is that good, and acceptable, and perfect, will of God."

Presenting our bodies as living sacrifices to God is the first thing we are to do with every single day of our lives. We may do it in a time of private prayer or meditation, while driving to work, or in the midst of the daily tasks that confront us. But knowingly, we must daily give away that part of life which is ours to God. God directs and blesses only what we give Him; everything else goes undirected and unblessed.

Psychologists tell us that the people who grow old gracefully and fully are, by and large, people who have lived each stage of life fully. We are prone to always live in the future, never quite content with today.

Jesus warned against being overly anxious about all the tomorrows in such a way that we ruin the present. We should regard each day as a gift we have received, and are in turn offering back to God for His blessing. No one receives a gift, puts it in the closet, and never opens it. Yet many people deal with life that way. They receive each day of life and allow it to remain an unopened gift, an unblessed gift. Gradually life becomes a closet of unopened gifts—an accumulation of yesterdays which were never really lived. Yet all our yesterdays are gone forever; the only things we can store up are the opened gifts, the days we have received and offered back to God. These days become our treasure, our memories, and our reward. When we give each day to God we allow Him to direct it according to His will, thus we remain open throughout the hours of that day to the fact that God may intervene in some ordinary experience and impress us to touch the life of someone else in a healing way.

Keep your identity. Identity is based on relationships, and the Christian is one who has found a new relationship of peace with God. Hence Scripture warns about being "conformed to this world." The world, meaning the world of men apart from God, is ever trying to blend everyone in together. But the word *conformed* contains the root word that has to do with one's outward form that varies from year to year, according to the pressures applied, or the popularities of the moment. It has to do with the manner in which one beholds himself. It often refers to the adoption or the imitation of some mode of conduct. Paul's warning is against trying to live like the chameleon, that blends in with whatever is current.

Before some people can answer the question "Who am I?" they often have to stop and take into account their latest hero, the latest book they have read, or the latest movie they have seen. In trying to be everything and everybody a person becomes nothing and nobody. Only by maintaining self-identity as a child of God can one live the truth.

No one who has a great future wants to swap names and I.D. cards. To avoid letting this happen, the Christian is urged to "be transformed by the renewing of your mind." This is the alternative to being poured into the world's mold. Each of us will change during life in one way or another. Change will either be divinely directed, and come from within; or it will be directed by the pressures of society.

A successful businessman and friend once told me of his own experience of trying to change. Having just divorced his wife, he decided he didn't like himself very well and sought help from a psychiatrist. His main request of the psychiatrist was that he be given shock treatments in an effort to change his personality. The doctor gave him some assurance that such a procedure could succeed, but warned him that it might make him a vegetable.

The troubled man signed the necessary papers and took six weeks of agonizing shock treatments. He described the experience as "like being electrocuted over and over again." When the treatments were over, he was indeed a vegetable. His parents found out where he was and came to take him home with them to take care of him. He could still recognize faces, but remembered little more. He could talk only in monosyllables. Hearing the doctor tell his parents that he would never be any better, he determined that the doctor would not be right. By sheer determination he recovered. As he related this experience to me, he said, "And now, here is the joke: when I recovered I found that I was exactly the same person I had been in the beginning." This man went on to tell me that he found nothing which brought him any sense of fulfillment. Business, sex, and possessions had come to have little satisfaction at all. He said his search was for something that would bring fulfillment to his life.

This friend's major problem was that, because of a disillusioning experience in a church years before, he had by and large shut God out of his life. It was not that he did not believe in God, but rather that he had determined never to be involved with Him again in the context of worship, church, or service. An additional reason that kept him from ever wanting to be involved again, was that it would require changing his total lifestyle—one he had come to enjoy very much. Yet at that moment in time he was a miserable person. As he shared this experience with me, tears came into his eyes. He is a kind, sensitive, caring person, yet he holds God at a distance and thereby holds truth at a distance. He had not yet realized that there is no fulfillment apart from living the truth, and that the truth involves relating life and its experiences to the lordship of Jesus Christ. My friend was afraid of being "transformed" by the living Lord; he was afraid of the truth. The literal word used for "transformed" is the word from which we get metamorphosis. This is the process by which a worm in a cocoon becomes a beautiful butterfly—in a natural way.

Dare to experience the new. To allow God to work change in your life requires that you be willing to live with the insecurity of new experiences. Christian growth demands this. Keith Miller in his book, *The Becomers*, speaks of Christian growth in terms of one who is becoming a useful Christian. Miller sees Christian growth in terms of a continuing surrender of our securities about us. Abraham was asked to leave all his securities and travel to a new land. As Abraham was willing to turn loose of his securities and follow God, he experienced spiritual growth. The apostle Paul was asked to turn loose of his pharisaical securities which marked him as one of the leaders in Judaism, and to step in faith to a new life in Jesus Christ. Salvation not only begins in faith; it grows and matures as one continues to exercise faith by turning loose of the securities he is constantly accumulating. Pierre Teilhard de Chardin speaks of this kind of relinquishment and says it is a perfect preparation for death when the Christian is called upon to make the final surrender of all in which he feels secure.

Paul Tournier sees life's risks in terms of the trapeze artist who must turn loose of his trapeze if he is to grasp the other one that is swung toward him. Otherwise he merely swings back and forth in the same place.

When we turn loose of our surroundings in which we feel comfortable, and dare to make life an adventure of faith, we put God's will to the test. The only way one can "prove what is that good and acceptable and perfect will of God" is by daring to live it.

When Moses decided to turn loose of his security as the heir to the throne of Egypt, he was making a choice that would not be shown correct for years. Indeed, only as an old man could the world at last see that the bargain he made was the right one. In the meantime he had made hundreds of other choices that awaited verification by time.

William Ernest Hocking, the Harvard philosopher of years gone by, said, "Only religion can create the unpurchasable man. And it is only the man unpurchasable by society who can create a sound society." Our Lord wants us to know the joy of living a life that is not prostituted to the highest bidder. To stand in the earth as one who is committed to Christ, and who is willing to live out life—to put it to the test—is daring to live the truth.

NOTES

1. Samuel Shumaker, *Under New Managemant* (Grand Rapids: Zondervan Publishing House, 1966), p. 136.
2. John G. Williams, *Christian Faith in the Space Age* (Cleveland: The World Publishing Co., 1968), p. 70.

Whosoever will be chief among you,
let him be your servant:
Even as the Son of man came
not to be ministered unto,
but to minister. . . .
(Matt. 20:27, 28)

9

Give Yourself Away

■Our Lord said, "It is more blessed to give than to receive," but the human nature within us asks, "Is giving really necessary?" Each of us has obligations to provide for his family, and to this end the average person devotes most of his earthly life. We do not question the necessity of working to provide for our needs. But we wonder if it is as necessary to give, as it is to get. Giving puts no food on our tables or clothes on our backs. It does not increase our securities in the bank. Why isn't it enough merely to have faith in God, and to work hard?

The answer is quite simple. Unless we learn the principle of total giving, we shall measure our lives in terms of our own efforts and accomplishments. When we see others who are doing less work, we will indulge in self-pity because we have given so much more than they have. The antidote to self-pity is to learn the meaning of total giving, and to realize that it is in the giving of ourselves that we discover life. For this reason our Lord affirmed, "For whosoever will save his life, shall lose it. But whosoever will lose his life, for my sake, the same shall find it." Those who give all, gain all.

Toward the end of His earthly ministry, our Lord once explained to His disciples that He was going to Jerusalem to give Himself on the cross. Simon Peter interrupted Him and said, "This shall not be unto thee" (Matt. 16:22). Peter actually meant, "I don't believe you should give that much." Our Lord looked at him and said, "Get behind me, Satan." In Peter's words and attitude our Lord heard the sinister voice of Satan, who is the author of all selfishness.

And so the concept of giving one's self away comes from the life of the Lord Himself, as Paul writes: "For you know the grace of our Lord Jesus Christ, that, though he was rich, yet for your sakes he became poor, that you through his poverty might be rich" (II Cor. 8:9).

We speak much about the grace of God, but I wonder if we actually understand what is involved. We use the word *grace* when we talk of all that God gives us, but I think it is important to understand the basic concept of grace: God offers us Himself. In fact, He already has given Himself to us. Think about this for a moment. We talk of finding the new life in Christ, of His forgiveness, and of being saved by the grace of God. In times of trial we speak of being strengthened by the grace of God. What we mean is that God *gives us His presence*. He walks along beside us, and thus gives us power.

God's giving of Himself is His way of letting us know

He cares. I once read a story about an Italian journalist who had followed the writing career of Sinclair Lewis for many years. Eventually, he was able to arrange an interview with Lewis. The journalist discussed with Lewis his writing reputation, and they talked about such works as *Babbitt* and *Main Street* in which Lewis had pointed out inequities and moral failures in certain areas of American life. The journalist then asked if, after exposing these weaknesses, Lewis had any solution for them. To this Lewis replied, "I have no answers, and what's more, I don't care!" The journalist went back and wrote in his column: "Sinclair Lewis is a great writer but he is not a great man, because great men care." We never learn to care until we come to the place we are willing to give.

We all have certain basic needs that can be met only by our determination to become people who give. Faith itself is a decision to give ourselves to the heavenly Father. And every human relationship must be based on the willingness to give, or it will be doomed to deterioration and failure. In Jesus' parable of the prodigal son, the elder brother's chief problem was that, having heard his father say, "All that I have is thine," he was not prepared to repeat, "and all that *I* have is thine." As a result the relationship between father and son was strained.

Since our faith in God begins with giving, the growth of that relationship requires a growth in our willingness to give ourselves away in His name. Otherwise we remain like children who try to get away with doing the bare minimum. The child who is told to wash his face will often ask, "Do I have to wash my ears, too?" When told to mow the yard, a child will often ask, "Do I have to mow the back yard, too?" In school, when told to write a five-page essay, the student will often ask, "May I double space?" The mark of immaturity is the desire to get by on the minimum requirement. Such practice produces minimal living. There are some very important reasons why each of us needs to become a giver.

GIVING BRINGS PURPOSE TO LIFE

The decision to become a person who gives brings a sense of purpose to life. Life is incomplete as long as it is filled only with our efforts to achieve, to accumulate, and to possess. Once we begin the process of accumulation, we are like the rich man in the parable as he looked at his barns full of grain and pondered his next move. His solution was that he should build more barns so he could have more grain stored away. The Scripture calls him a fool for such a decision. He did not realize that there should be two basic aspects of life—the getting and the giving.

Paul Tournier, the noted Christian psychiatrist, explains that acquiring is important; it is the first movement of life. But if a person has done nothing but acquire he still has not had the most fundamental experience of life, which is what Tournier calls the second movement. This movement has to do with giving away what one has acquired. Man comes to the turning point in his life when he freely lets go of what he has received; the failure to do so will make him the prisoner of his own possessions. It will also make rather meaningless the acquisition of possessions. For this reason Scripture warns, "A man's life does not consist of the abundance of the things which he possesses" (Luke 12:15). A person who breathes in must also learn to breathe out.[1] It is a part of the rhythm of life.

One who labors and acquires is incomplete until he has learned to give. Try doing nothing but breathing in for a while and see what happens.

When the apostle Paul was trying to help some of the young Christians in the church at Corinth, he wrote a rather pointed criticism of their lifestyle. They were trying to live as Christians without taking any risks. He noted that they were surrounded by blessings, proud of their personal accomplishments, and in fact living like kings in a world filled with great need. Listen to him: "Now you are full, now you are rich, you have reigned as kings without us" (I Cor. 4:8). The Corinthians had not learned the secret of giving. Paul realized that unless this condition were corrected they would never discover the real purpose of life.

Purpose comes as we are willing to accept as our own personal responsibilities the needs that we see about us. Happiness is never found in avoiding responsibilities, but in accepting them and giving oneself to them. James Buckingham tells about an old grandfather clock which was one of his father's cherished possessions. Winding the clock every Sunday morning was a kind of family ritual. All the children would stand around their father as he opened the long glass door and wound the clock with a big key. The children would watch in fascination as the heavy weight which had slowly descended during the week was wound back up by the key. When James was eight years old, he was home by himself one day and he noticed the heavy weight which had descended about halfway down the huge pendulum. Deciding the clock must be weary, he opened the forbidden glass door and unhooked the weight, putting it on the floor. He thought the clock could now rest for the remainder of the week.

Then something happened! The pendulum slowed to a stop. The ticking stopped. The hands stopped moving. James tried to rehook the weight but his small fingers couldn't make it fit. The rest of the afternoon was spent fearing his father's return. When he explained what he had done, the father went to the clock and gently replaced the weight. He reset the hands and put the pendulum in motion. The ticking and tocking started up again. Then the father sat down on the bottom step and pulled Buckingham close to his side. He explained the workings of the clock, and with his arms around his son said, "Remember, Jamie, it's the weight that keeps the clock going."[2]

As paradoxical as it may seem, our greatest burdens and sacrifices are often the source of our deepest joys. This is illustrated in the parable of Sadhu Sundar Singh, a Hindu convert to Christianity who then became a missionary in India. Late one winter evening Sadhu was traveling on foot through the Himalayas accompanied by a Buddhist monk. As night drew on and the bitter cold intensified, the monk warned Sadhu that they were in danger of freezing to death unless they soon reached the monastery.

As they traversed the narrow path above a steep precipice they heard a cry for help. Looking over the cliff, Sadhu saw a man who had fallen and was badly hurt. When the monk saw that Sadhu planned to try to assist the man, he warned, "Don't stop. God has brought this man to his fate. He must work it out for himself. Unless we hurry, we too shall perish."

But Sadhu, the Christian, replied, "God has sent me here to help my brother. I cannot abandon him." The monk continued off into the night through the swirling snow toward the monastery while Sadhu climbed down into the chasm, made a sling of his blanket, and tied the man on his back. Then, bending under the heavy burden, he began a painstaking climb back to the path. When at least he reached it, he was drenched with perspiration. He made his way doggedly through the deepening snow. Now it was totally dark and it was all he could do to follow the path. At last he saw ahead of him the faint lights of the monastery. At that moment he stumbled and almost fell, not from weakness, but because of some object lying in the road. Brushing the snow off the object he discovered it was the body of the Buddhist monk, frozen to death. Years later, when a disciple of Sadhu's asked him, "What is life's most difficult task?" Sadhu replied without hesitation: "To have no burden to carry."[3]

Martin Buber, the theologian-philosopher, claims there are two kinds of people—image people and essence people. Image people concern themselves almost entirely with the impression they are making on others. They are like little children who try to gain attention by performing. In contrast, essence people simply give of themselves, knowing that the basic responsibility in life is to respond. The widow whom Jesus saw dropping in her last two pennies, the woman who anointed Jesus with the expensive flask of alabaster ointment, and Barnabas who sold his land and gave the money to the church were all people who had learned that the basic response in life is giving. They were essence people. What they did was not done with a desire to impress others, but was in fact a genuine response of the heart. Their acts brought purpose to their lives.

Sometime ago Roger Kahn wrote a book entitled, *The Boys of Summer*, a story about the Brooklyn Dodgers in the 1950s. But it is more than a story about baseball; it is a story about the meaning of life. Kahn writes about several of the best-known members of the famous Brooklyn Dodger team of the 1950s and what happened to them in the twenty years that followed their fame. He talks about how a ball player has to confront two deaths—first his death as an athlete, and then later physical death. By retracing the steps of those men after their glory days were over, Kahn shows how for each of them their happiness had ended. Who will ever remember these once-mighty men? It is a sad book and the sobering question that comes out of it is simply, "Where is the life we have lost in the living?" The decision to be a giver brings lasting purpose to life and prevents us from having to look back on our own years and realize they were wasted in selfishness.

GIVING SATISFIES OUR NEED
FOR INVESTMENT

We all feel the need to invest in something, and we are frustrated until we decide what that investment will be. We see life rushing by and realize we need to be spending ourselves on something. The greatest investment in all of life is to invest in people, because people are made in the image of God.

Carol Burnett tells about an anonymous benefactor who gave her one thousand dollars when he learned of her desire to go to New York and try to get into show business. He made two stipulations. She was never to tell anyone his name, and if she was successful she was in turn to anonymously help someone else. She went to

New York with that thousand dollars and the rest is history.

Each of us has been enriched in some way or other by the investment others have made in our lives. There is something deep within us that will never be satisfied until we, too, begin to make investments in the lives of others.

Our Lord once said that even the giving of a mere cup of water in His name would be blessed. He spoke of the coming judgment as a time when He would say to His followers, "Come, ye blessed of my Father, inherit the kingdom prepared for you from the foundations of the world: I was thirsty, and ye gave me drink: I was a stranger, and ye took me in: naked, and ye clothed me: I was sick, and ye visited me: I was in prison, and ye came unto me" (Matt. 25:34–36).

Our Lord continued by saying that many would wonder when they ever did all of those things for the Lord. Christ explained, "And the King shall answer and say unto them, Verily I say unto you, Inasmuch as you have done it unto one of the least of these my brethren, you have done it unto me" (Matt. 25:40). We are born to give. Happiness is found only when we take the risk of giving.

We have a choice between two arenas in which to live life. In one we participate in what never fades, and in the other we participate with the knowledge that everything done is temporary. We have a choice between the kingdom of God and this earth. One is the world in which everything meaningful can be taken with us; the other is the world in which everything dear must some day be left behind. Whether we realize it or not, we do make investments—all of us do. If we invest only in ourselves, we live small, selfish lives. If we decide to give, to invest in the lives of others, and in the purposes of God, we discover a life of joy.

Jesus once warned (literally): "Stop treasuring up earthly treasures and start treasuring up heavenly treasures (Matt. 6:19–20). This is a call to choose carefully what we shall accumulate in life. It also points out the impossibility of using earthly treasures to store up eternal rewards. Earthly treasures are not evil in themselves, but they are always uncertain. They are never the basis on which to build life. Heavenly treasures permit us an opportunity to make an investment in the things that are eternal.

Paul Tournier relates a dream that he finds recurring again and again in the lives of those who come to him for help. In the dream, the person finds himself trying to catch this train, yet without knowing why it is that he must do so. He begins to run, makes desperate efforts, and finds himself hindered by his luggage. Terror mounts as he sees he is about to miss the train. Oftentimes the dreamer finds the train going by just in front of him. Sometimes he is lucky enough to be able to jump on board, only to realize that it is the wrong train, or that there is no room for him inside.[4] The dream reveals our hunger to find meaning in life. This meaning always eludes us as long as our only desire is to treasure up for ourselves treasures on earth. Genuine purpose comes to us only as we are willing to use what we are, and what we have, for others.

Scripture talks about the need for self-denial, but self-denial is not a virtue in and of itself. In fact, self-denial can be utterly selfish. We can deny ourselves things so that we may ultimately have more things for ourselves. Self-denial has meaning only as we do it to truly follow Christ.

If we follow Christ we must become a giver, for our Lord gave all.

However, we need to make an important distinction. If we give only with the thought of laying up eternal rewards we have not yet learned the meaning of giving. We must become people who give because we desire to be genuinely helpful and useful in this earth. The very act of giving then becomes its own reward. It is in the process of giving that we come to have a healthy appreciation for ourselves; we recognize that the bonds of selfishness have been broken.

GIVING IS NECESSARY FOR PERSONAL GROWTH

The good news that comes from God is that we can become new people through faith in Him. However, faith is only the beginning of a journey. If we are to grow in this newness which is offered to us in Christ, we must be givers, not just receivers. The big mistake which Adam made in the Garden of Eden was that, for a moment, he saw himself as god of the garden rather than as its caretaker. Our natural tendency is to make of our life a little kingdom in which we reign as god. It is only by giving that we keep our proper perspective in life.

Harvey Cox uses the term "social catalepsy" to speak of a kind of paralysis which keeps people from facing up to new challenges. Catalepsy itself is a disease characterized by muscular rigidity and paralysis. When man is confronted by the gospel of Christ, he must either repent, or cling to "this dying age." Cox says that the reason many seem paralyzed by this confrontation is that they have become too much a part of the world of things.[5] To become a person who gives himself away is an awesome thought. We stand on the brink, and we grow no more until we step into the chasm of needs all about us, where people are struggling in life. We must listen to the call of God's kingdom, and determine that this is the end for which we were born and to which we must give ourselves. All else is paralysis.

We are our own worst enemy at the moment of decision to become a giver. In Victor Hugo's immortal work, Jean Valjean cries out in anguish, "It is I myself who bar the way before myself, and I drag myself, and I urge myself, and I check myself, and I exert myself, and when one holds himself he is well-held."[6]

Giving allows us to escape ourselves. On April 25, 1975, the London branch of the Bank of America was robbed. Six armed gunmen gained entrance to the underground strongroom where vaults and deposit boxes were located. It was estimated that they escaped with over seven million dollars in valuables from customers' safety deposit boxes. Many of the patrons of that bank were wealthy American celebrities. One lady, who had over a half million dollars in jewelry in her box, exclaimed: "Everything I've got was in there. My whole life was in that box!" What haunting words! When we determine to be people who give ourselves away, we escape the imprisonment of ourselves. We avoid the possibility of ever having to make the statement made by that woman.

The ancient pharoahs of Egypt were buried in their great pyramids, surrounded by gold, jewels, clothing, and food. They died surrounded by their dead gods, sealed in a tomb with their dead gods, and grave robbers later found their skeletons rotting amid their dead gods. I remember a man in a town where I once lived who, on a much smaller scale, followed the same philosophy of life. Though not a wealthy man by any stretch of the imagination, he had given his life to accumulating earthly treasures. He lived in a small house and had iron bars placed over all the windows, for he kept everything he possessed in that small house. One night, while he slept, his house caught fire. Awakening too late, he was unable to get to the door. The firemen who came were unable to get into the windows because of the iron bars. Everything he had was in that small house, which was built like a prison, and all perished with him. The dimensions of his life were terribly small. He had shut himself in and made his own tomb.

George Buttrick, in speaking of the foolish man in Scripture whose goal in life was nothing more than building more and larger barns, observes that each person must keep a proper distance between himself and his possessions. Buttrick affirms that a person must say to his possessions: "You are not my life. You can never be my life. There is a gulf set between you and me."[7] It is only by the process of becoming a giver that one is able to stand apart from his possessions, to be an individual with them or without them. It is at this point he is able to become a real person, to live as an individual, to grow and develop in the newness of faith in Christ.

THE EQUATION FOR GIVING

Too often we make the mistake of assuming that others can become givers, but not us. We think we have nothing to give. We may believe that our personality is so poverty-stricken that no one could be blessed by our encouragement, or we may believe that our finances are so limited that we could never be a help materially to anyone else, or even to the kingdom of God.

However, Scripture gives a most remarkable mathematic equation for giving. The apostle Paul once held up the people in the churches of Macedonia as an example of genuine giving. Although the churches of Macedonia had not been blessed with great wealth, yet they had become an example of liberality. Notice the equation found in Scripture as the apostle Paul describes their activity of giving: "In a great trial of affliction the abundance of their joy and their deep poverty abounded unto the riches of their liberality" (II Cor. 8:2). The equation, then, is that severe trials brought about by affliction, plus deep poverty, plus abundant joy, equals the riches of liberality.

Now it is common sense that trials and severe poverty do not abound, or overflow, in riches. The key is found in the word "joy." This is the overflowing which, even though it was mingled with great affliction and deep poverty, brought about a rich liberality in giving. The word *joy* used here is the word used for happiness which God's saving grace gives to a person's heart. Those who have this joy are those who have made contact with heaven. Such an overflowing sense of joy and gratitude is able to overrule the deepest of deprivations, the most severe poverty, and abound into a gracious style of living that is marked by liberality. Those who can afford to give of themselves are those who, in spite of trials and poverty, have experienced an overflowing joy in their hearts and lives because of what Christ has done for them. Each of us has much to give. God did not make us to be useless. He made us for purpose, for blessing, for giving.

At this point we need to take seriously the words of our Lord when He said: "Whosoever will save his life will lose it: but whosoever will lose his life for my sake shall find it" (Matt. 16:25). We have the option of "saving our life." This means we can build a wall around it, enclose it in a prison, strangle it with selfishness, and thereby lose it. The other alternative is to take the daring risk of giving it away in Christ's name. God can only bless what we give, and this is the blessing that produces joy and happiness which is no longer dependent on outward circumstances.

Recently there was a television program entitled "Eric," which told the true story of a young man who died of leukemia. Previously I had read an article about him in *Reader's Digest* in which his mother told the heart-rending story of his battle with the dreaded disease. She talked of how Eric endured and survived so many crises before the end came. She talked of how he "learned to live on the ledge and not look down."

A few days before he died, he talked with his mother about all the good things in his life—the way he felt about his sisters and the wonderful times he had had with his brothers. He recalled how he loved those times when he could run on the beach. He talked about his love of life and the beautiful world he had enjoyed so much. As he grew tired that evening, he said to his mother, "Do something for me. Leave a little early. Walk a few blocks. Look at the sky, and walk in the world for me. . . ."

There is a real sense in which our Lord, as He stood with His disciples just before He ascended into heaven, said the same thing. He told them they would receive power from the Holy Spirit. Then He added, "And you shall be witnesses unto me . . . unto the uttermost part of the earth." Christ was saying to His disciples what He says to every person: "Walk in the world for me."

Our Lord calls us to begin our journey of faith with the awareness that we must live a lifestyle which walks in the world for Him. In the process we discover that to walk for Him means we must also walk for others who have burdens too heavy to bear, hurts too deep to heal, and needs too large to be met. Life is a calling to give, and we must give to others Christ's healing love.

Take a moment and do a quiet inventory of all your relationships. Do you really dare to give yourself to your friends? How about your enemies? Have you ever really tried doing something helpful for someone who has mistreated you? Have you ever tried giving back good where only evil has been received? What about strangers you meet day in and day out? Are you willing to give yourself to your spouse, or do you operate with ulterior motives and a desire to have your spouse always give to you what you want? Do you really give yourself to your children, or do you merely look upon them as responsibilities and possessions? Why not tear down the fences, remove all the outer shells which protect you, and dare to give yourself? That is when life is discovered.

NOTES

1. Paul Tournier, *A Place for You* (New York: Harper and Row, 1968), pp. 144–45.

2. James Buckingham, *Some Gall and Other Reflections on Life* (Waco, TX: Word Books, 1970), pp. 63–65.

3. From *Bits and Pieces* (December, 1976), p. 18.

4. Tournier, pp. 34–37.

5. Harvey Cox, *The Secular City* (New York: MacMillan, 1965), pp. 101–102.

6. Victor Hugo, *Les Miserables* (New York: Random House, n.d.), pp. 1168–69.

7. George Buttrick, *The Parables of Jesus* (Grand Rapids: Baker Book House, 1973), pp. 131–2.

Lay up for yourselves treasures
in heaven, where neither moth
nor rust doth corrupt, and where
thieves do not break through nor steal:
For where your treasure is,
there will your heart be also.
(Matt. 6:20–21)

10

Discover the Meaning of Work and Play

■Is a man a good man simply because he works hard? Is he lazy if he takes time off? Are weekends to be used as one pleases? What claim does Christ have on a Christian's work time and leisure time?

Paul reminded Timothy that God has given us "all things to enjoy" (I Tim. 6:17), and the Talmud quotes Abba Areka as stating, "On the day of reckoning man will have to give an account of every good which his eyes beheld and which he did not enjoy." But all of God's gifts are open to misuse. We need a clear understanding of work and leisure as they relate to our search for wholeness.

A CHRISTIAN VIEW OF WORK

J. Edward Carothers says that there are only four things that may be appropriately done by a human being—work, play, worship, and love.[1] By the time we reach retirement we will have worked one hundred twenty-five thousand hours, providing we work forty hours a week. Thus, work is a very important subject for the Christian.

Work is ordained of God; it is not a curse growing out of man's sin in the Garden of Eden. When Adam was created and placed in the garden he was given the responsibility of caring for the garden. The curse that came upon man because of his sin was not that man would now have to work, but rather that he would have to work in loneliness and separation from God.

Labor is not something to be avoided. Dr. Albert Schweitzer tells of his experience while building his hospital in Lambarene, French Equatorial Africa. On one occasion he was carrying a heavy beam and desperately needed help. He called to a native who was dressed in a white suit and had just been visiting a friend who was a hospital patient. The native, feeling insulted, refused to help by explaining that he was an intellectual (as though work is something to be done only by the lowly and uneducated). Schweitzer, with earned doctorates in theology, music, and medicine, answered the native by saying that he always had wished he could have been an intellectual, but apparently had failed.

Charles Jones tells about a man who dreamed he inherited a million dollars. In the dream, he got up bright and early to take a shower, but the shower wouldn't shower. He plugged in his electric razor and nothing happened. Neither would his electric coffee pot or toaster work. Going outside to buy a newspaper he discovered that the newspaper wasn't available. Deciding to catch a bus and go uptown, he discovered that the buses had stopped running. After forty-five minutes a man came walking down the street with the answer to all the dilemmas. His statement was: "Haven't you heard? Everybody's inherited a million dollars! Nobody's working anymore!"[2]

The man who has work to do should never be embarrassed about it but should rather rejoice in the opportunity of it. Dorothy Sayers observes that the essential heresy of our Christian society's view of work is that it identifies work with gainful employment; the result being that wheat and coffee are often burned, and fish are used for manure while other populations starve to death. In other words, work is looked upon as something a man does in order to obtain money and earn leisure time, rather than a creative energy done in the service of society.

A well-known surgeon said no one works merely to get a job done. The result of the work seems to be only a by-product. The aim of the work is to make money in order to be able to do something else. Often doctors practice medicine, not primarily to relieve suffering, but to make a good living. A cured patient is merely a by-product. Lawyers often accept briefs, not because of their passion for justice, but because by doing so they earn a good living. Similar analogies can be made in every profession.

The man who proposes to live meaningfully must discover the spiritual dimension of work. Jesus said, "I must work the works of Him that sent me while it is yet day, for the night cometh when no man can work." He called men to follow Him because if they could see what He was about, they would be able to see the way of life through His eyes.

Though work is ordained by God, it is not to be deified. In Dorothy Sayer's play, *The Zeal of Thy House*, she warns against making work more important than the Lord who gives us the opportunity to work. Toward the end of that play, William, the master architect, is told that he has sinned through his work. At first he cannot believe such is possible, but then he begins to understand that he has placed his work, and his pride in his work, above God. He then observes, "The work was not ill done—'twas done too well."

Many are in the process of working themselves to death, supposing that by doing so they are pleasing God. They feel guilty if they are not working every moment. And the more they come to possess, the more they feel they must work. The thought of leisure time threatens them. Such a philosophy may leave a person with no time left for living. Work is an opportunity to provide the needs of one's family, to contribute to the general welfare of humanity, and to build up the kingdom of God, but work is not the only dimension of life.

A CHRISTIAN VIEW OF LEISURE

While work is ordained of God, leisure is as well. God rested from His creation and decreed that one day of seven be set aside as a day of rest. Jesus often withdrew from the crowds to private places where He could rest with His disciples. A time for rest is a gift of God, just as the opportunity to work is a gift of God. Both can be misused.

Today, many people are trapped by leisure time and feel they should perform as others do. My mother and father, recently retired, have gone through some of the problems that many others have. Because all their friends had bought travel trailers on retirement, they assumed they were obligated to do the same. Neither of them like to travel or camp, yet they bought a travel trailer. Their total use of it in the last year and a half has been one trip to Lake Texoma where, after going through all the motions of getting the trailer blocked up and leveled, they spent one night and then came home the next day.

An anonymous friar at a monastery in Nebraska wrote:

> If I had my life to live over, I'd try to make more mistakes next time. I would relax, I would limber up, I would be sillier than I have been this trip. I know of a very few things I would take seriously. I would be less hygienic. I would take more chances. I would take more trips. I would climb more mountains, swim more rivers, and watch more sunsets. I would eat more ice cream. I would have actual troubles and fewer imaginary ones.

> You see, I am one of those people who lives prophylactically and sensibly and sanely, hour after hour, day after day. Oh, I've had my moments and, if I had it to do over again, I'd have more of them. In fact, I'd try to have nothing else. Just moments, one after another, instead of living so many years ahead each day. I have been one of those people who never go anywhere without a thermometer, a hot water bottle, a gargle, a rain coat, and a parachute. If I had it to do over again, I would go places and do things and travel lighter than I have. . . .[3]

Leisure is an opportunity for experiences of eternity. Leisure is a time when one can experience freedom in

Christ, can define himself in his own role in life, and can set up his own boundaries before the world comes in and takes over. Leisure is man's one chance to disengage himself from the assembly line mechanization which surrounds us and reach out for something that is "out of this world."[4]

Leisure should not be looked on as a recess from working. Neither should it be considered a reward for working—a time of self-gratification and extravagance. Leisure is an existence that is free of coercion or restraint. Leisure and freedom are very similar, yet leisure time is not merely free time. Our leisure time reveals the direction of our life and the place of our values.

Ibsen tells how Peer Gynt sought to discover himself and was dismayed to learn that he was like an onion— that one layer after the other could be peeled off and no core could be found. This is the experience of every man whose life is void of a spiritual dimension.

Leisure is an opportunity to give purpose to life. It is quite possible to learn more about a person's deep sense of purpose in life by what he does with his leisure time than by what he does on the job. Many people are not provileged to have a daily work that grants them a sense of accomplishment and fulfillment. In Arthur Miller's play, *Death of a Salesman*, Willie Loman's son, speaking at the grave of his ill-fated father, said, "He never knew who he was." Especially for such people, leisure time is an opportunity to have a purpose and to spend some time in pursuing it.

Leisure time can become a curse unless it has some purpose. Jesus told a parable about a rich farmer who, in the midst of his financial success, said to himself: "Take thine ease, eat, drink, and be merry." Thus his one goal is revealed—the amassing of treasures on earth. Jesus said the man was not "rich toward God"—his goals were too limited. This use of leisure causes people to live in a world of need, yet ignore the masses about them. The waste some bring to their leisure time would be akin to the Boston Symphony Orchestra assembling on a stage before a filled house, tuning up its instruments, and playing "Pop Goes the Weasel."[5] Leisure time allows a person time for himself, time for his family, and time for God.

REQUIRES A CHRISTIAN VIEW OF VOCATION

To have a proper understanding of work and leisure requires an understanding of the concept of Christian vocation. The apostle Paul admonishes, "walk worthy of the vocation wherewith you are called" (Eph. 4:1). The Christian is one who recognizes that his calling is a full-time experience.

Gives meaning to menial tasks. There are millions of people at work today whose only purpose is to put in a bolt or tighten a nut on an assembly line. It is difficult for these workers to go home at the end of the day and feel like they have personally accomplished anything. But as they approach these menial tasks as Christian disciples, their work takes on meaning.

To become a Christian is to join a fellowship. The word *fellowship* originally came from the business world and had to do with partners who pledged joint efforts in a business venture on which they staked their future and their families. Israel as a people had a corporate vocation—they were to be the instrument of God by which He would reveal Himself to the world, and thus bless the world. The Christian joins a fellowship with this same kind of corporate calling as he becomes a part of the church.

Therefore, the man who puts one screw in each machine that passes by him on the assembly line can find meaning if he uses his work as an opportunity to be a witness for Christ. Whereas his specific task may be rather meaningless, he does it in the midst of a multitude of others who need spiritual direction and the good news of the Gospel. Being a Christian witness is indeed one's vocation.

Paul made tents but he never looked on tent-making as his major task in life. Jesus was a carpenter, but His work was finished only when He had finished the divine work that God intended (John 17:4). Every Christian has a divine task which is his basic work (John 6:29; John 14:12). Just as a stockbroker studies the market in an effort to make the best purchase for his client, the Christian must study his opportunities and determine to perform the best spiritual service. This makes the Christian faith both a sanctuary and a battle station. Man is in the world, not to flee from it, but to redeem it.

A search for real riches. The Christian is called on to seek out the deepest riches of life: "Charge them that are rich in this world, that they be not high-minded, nor trust in uncertain riches, but in the living God, who giveth us richly all things to enjoy: That they do good, that they be rich in good works, ready to distribute, willing to communicate; Laying up in store for themselves a good foundation against the time to come, that they may lay hold on eternal life" (I Tim. 6:17–19).

Allow the Lordship of Christ over all of life. As long as we try to separate work and leisure, we will have problems with our priorities. Dorothy Sayers reminds us that one of the essential heresies of our time is that, for most of us, work is identified with what we do for gainful employment. Work is what we do for money; the chief goal being that we at last arrive at a place where we no longer have to work because we no longer need money. A proper understanding of the Christian vocation of life requires that we understand that both our labor and our leisure are wrapped up in our commitment to Christ and each is to glorify Him. There should never be the kind of separation between work and leisure that causes some to thumb their nose at God each weekend, supposing that those days are theirs.

Leisure may well afford one an opportunity to accomplish that for which he was born. A Christian following his vocation realizes that his major work is to stand alongside his heavenly Father and bring meaning and creation out of imperfection. For this reason, I always worry a little about people who, caught up in the frantic anxieties of life, decide the answer to their problem is to cut down on what they are doing for God in the church. This may well be the only meaningful thing in which they are involved.

Paul Tournier, the noted Christian physician and author, in his study on aging, suggests that increased leisure time be channeled in a purposeful way so that one can study and pursue those areas of personal improvement for which there has not been time before. This is not only the secret to retirement, but the secret to the use of leisure time. Leisure time permits us to free ourselves from the all-consuming task of making a living and to do those things which bring enjoyment, self-improvement, and deepen the possibilities of living out the Lord's will for life.

A proper view of the Christian vocation of life helps us

live for the moment instead of always living in the past or
in the future. There is a deep truth in the words of Walt
Kelly as he says: "Too soon we breast the tape, and too
late we realize the fun lay in the running. . . . If there be
any satisfaction in life it must come in transient, for who
can tell when he will be struck down in mid-method?"[6]

If Christ is lord of our lives, weekends are no longer
looked on as a way of escaping all responsibility, including God. Daily jobs no longer become an escape from all
thoughts of that which is above us and beyond us, of God
Himself. Rather, both the daily job, and the weekend of
leisure, come to be great opportunities to make, not a
better product, or a grander time, but to become a better
person in this earth, a more capable child of God, to
become more Christ-like, more compassionate, more joy-
ful in witness, more prayerful in meditation, more rested
physically, more aware of that which is eternal.

NOTES

1. J. Edward Carothers, "The Christian Meaning of Work,"
Religion and Labor, 4 (December-January, 1960−61): 1.

2. Charles E. Jones, *Life Is Tremendous* (Wheaton, IL: Tyn-
dale House Publishers, 1968), pp. 24−25.

3. John Killinger, *Bread for the Wilderness, Wine for the
Journey* (Waco, TX: Word Books, 1976), p. 69.

4. Gordon Dahl, "Time, Work and Leisure Today," *The
Christian Century* 88 (February 10, 1971): 187−88.

5. Rudolf Norden, *The Christian Encounters the New Leisure* (St. Louis: Concordia Publishing House, 1965), pp. 7−8.

6. Roy Pierson, *The Believer's Unbelief* (New York: Thomas
Nelson and Sons, 1963), pp. 36−37; 43−44.

Trust in the Lord with all thine heart;
and lean not unto thine own understanding
In all thy ways acknowledge him,
and he shall direct thy paths.
(Prov. 3:5, 6)

11
Learn to Trust

■Everything does not depend on you! Let that thought
sink in for a moment. Bask in the warm relief of it. You
can trust God with yourself, your loved ones, your career,
your future, your problems, your hurts—you can trust
God with everything!

From personal experience, the psalmist at last learned
this great truth: "Trust in the Lord with all thine heart; and
lean not unto thine own understanding." The psalmist
well defines trust in this simple statement. In Hebrew
poetry a statement is often followed by the same truth
stated in a different way which serves as an interpretation
or elaboration on the basic truth. To trust in the Lord is to
lean on Him rather than on your own self-sufficiency. To
trust is to depend upon, to place confidence in, to commit

something or someone to the care of another. To trust someone is to rely on that person. It is impossible to live without trust. Everyone, knowingly or not, trusts something or someone.

Since trust must always be based on performance, only God deserves our ultimate trust. Only He has never failed. Faith itself is the decision to trust Christ as Lord and Savior, to trust Him with your life. Faith is a daily "trusting" of yourself to Him in an ever-enlarging circle; every day you put more of your life in God's hands. Indeed, the ingredients of happiness require the trusting of God in every area of life. Since we are mortals, we have to stand in the shadow of someone larger than we. There is only one whose shadow complements rather than fragments us; God is the only one who allows our identity to be magnified rather than obliterated. To trust in the Lord is to stand in His shadow, which is "as the shadow of a great rock in a weary land" (Isa. 32:2).

To be sure, we must not only learn to trust God, but we must learn how to trust other human beings who are important to us. God is perfect. Everyone else we know is not. Therefore we need some guidelines, first of all on how to trust God, and second on how to trust the people around us who are important to us. Since all human trust must be an outgrowth of our trust in the heavenly Father, we shall first deal with our basic trust toward the Lord.

TRUST GOD FOR YOUR SPIRITUAL NEEDS

One of the great truths of the Scripture is that, in Christ, we have been adopted by the heavenly Father. Though we live in a world of displaced and lonely people, we live with assurance because we are a part of God's family. Out of this new relationship we draw our confidence: "For you have not received the spirit of bondage again to fear; but you have received the Spirit of *adoption*, whereby we cry, Abba, Father" (Rom. 8:15). The word "Abba" was a tender term used by children and could well be translated, "Daddy."

After the journey of faith has begun, we learn to trust our heavenly Father. He looks on us as His children, and He promises to watch over us with a power that knows no limits. We can say with the apostle Paul: "Being confident of this very thing, that he who has begun a good work in us will perform it until the day of Jesus Christ" (Phil. 1:6). What God begins He will complete.

We have many spiritual needs. We need forgiveness. We need a certainty about our eternal destination. We need help for the present problems of life. However, since we cannot erase our memories, there are times when our sins come back to haunt us and we wonder if indeed forgiveness is truly ours. There are times when our own human weakness leads us astray and we wonder if we really have become children of God.

While working on an Indian reservation directing vacation Bible schools and other such projects, our young people felt a real spiritual high. The whole project had been a great blessing to them. In the midst of those moments when emotions ran high, one of them asked our youth minister, "What are we going to do when we get back home? How will we keep this high so that we won't feel a letdown?" This brings up another question: Should a Christian feel victorious and deliriously happy every day of his life? While on the mission tour, the young people felt great assurance. Trust was easy. But they knew that when they came back home their feelings would cool off. Did this mean that their assurance would vanish with their enthusiasm?

Here we need to come to grips with an important truth. Trust cannot be based on *feelings*, because so many things affect the way we feel. Our feelings are affected by the weather, by what other people say, by what we do, by our own mistakes, by our health, and by a thousand other things. If we are able to trust God only when our feelings are exactly right, we shall be miserable most of our lives.

Trust in God must instead be based on facts. Feelings change. Facts do not. If we live by feelings, there will be times when we doubt our salvation, doubt that we are adopted into God's family. In an effort to speak to this problem, the apostle John writes: "These things have I written unto you that believe on the name of the Son of God; that you may know that you have eternal life" (I John 5:13). The facts of the Scripture are given to us to bring us assurance, and to deliver us from the frailty of our feelings. Listen again to the apostle John: "And this is the record, that God hath given to us eternal life, and this life is in his Son. He that hath the Son hath life; and he that hath not the Son of God hath not life" (I John 5:11–12). Notice that feeling is not mentioned. It is a fact that our salvation is a gift of God. It is a fact that we were adopted by God, and are kept by God (I Peter 1:5).

Trust can be experienced in spite of doubts, in the midst of doubts. The opposite of trust is not doubt. You can trust even amid doubts if you decide to do so. The Scripture tells us about one person who cried out: "Lord, I believe, help thou mine unbelief." He was trusting in spite of his doubts. The opposite of trust is emotional anxiety that clings, knots up, smothers, suspects, and fears. Jesus had this in mind when He warned: "Therefore be not anxious about tomorrow" (Matt. 6:34, my translation). To live, one must turn loose and trust God.

When we determine not to trust our feelings, but to trust God instead, we are simply facing our world realistically. We must recognize that we can't laugh all the time. We can't be healthy all the time. We can't be successful all the time. But we can decide to place our trust in God. We can decide to trust Him based on the fact that everything is in His hands. We may make wrong choices, we may regret certain deeds, we may fail in many areas, but God will not fail. God is not some kind of celestial "ski lift" who carries us to the top of a mountain every day so we can have the exhilarating joy of skiing downhill. But He has promised that He will never leave us nor forsake us, that His grace will be sufficient for every occasion.

Hebrews 11 describes the faithful people of biblical times. (Note that it, too, has nothing at all to say about feelings.) These people are held up as examples because they made decisions to trust God. They acted in spite of their doubts, not because they had none. Abraham must have had many doubts when God asked him to pull up his roots and follow Him into an unknown world. Moses must have had many doubts as God led him, first to forsake the throne of Egypt which could well have been his, and next to confront Pharaoh and lead the children of Israel out of bondage. Yet the great men and women of faith acted in the midst of their doubts. They decided to exercise trust. We, too, can decide to trust, and so participate in the divine plan of history.

Once we decide to trust, we can allow feelings to take care of themselves. Geoffrey Hoyland, in speaking of the importance of a quiet devotional time each day, calls it a "living silence." He reminds us that it is not easy to develop this kind of quiet in which we can accept the divine gift. However, he warns about relying on our feelings: "Above all we must avoid measuring the success of our communion by the emotional 'kick' we get out of it. Even if our emotions do not indicate that God is present, we know because of the promises of the Scripture that we belong to God and He belongs to us; we give ourselves to Him and He gives Himself to us, and there are no 'ifs' or 'buts' about it."[1]

When we are learning to trust God for our salvation, we must beware of stereotyping religious conversion. Recently I received a tragic letter from a troubled woman with many doubts. For five or six pages she shared different experiences in her search to place her faith in Jesus Christ. Each time, something her husband, or her pastor, or one of her friends had told her made her believe that she had never indeed placed her trust in God. In my response to her letter I tried to explain to her that God is not a master of hocus pocus. He does not perform some sleight of hand. He is not trying to deceive us. There are no secret bywords or formulas which must be stated exactly in order for us to become part of God's family. We come to Christ in childlike faith, with surrendered hearts and repentant spirits. The way that happens may depend on the circumstances and on our own personalities. P. T. Forsythe said he was converted the day he realized he was the object of God's grace. The Scripture tells us that Zacchaeus was up in a tree watching a parade when Christ looked up into the branches and asked him to come down. Zacchaeus responded as directed, and his life was changed. The thief on the cross merely asked, "Remember me when thou comest into thy kingdom." There are no set words which must be said. God simply calls us to come and walk by faith. Once we have made that decision, He calls us to walk daily by the same kind of faith. To do this we must learn to trust Him, to trust His promises of deliverance, His promises of forgiveness, His promises of divine providence. All is in His hands. We can decide to trust Him. And once we decide to accept the fact that everything depends on God, and that we can trust Him, we can relax. The basic decision has been made. Having learned that simple fact of trust, we can now enlarge the circle of trust until it includes every area of our lives.

TRUST GOD FOR YOUR SUCCESS

Each of us is afraid that somehow we are going to miss something in life. We are afraid that we will not accomplish what we should. We are afraid that we will fail. As long as we are convinced that everything depends on us, that we must climb to the top of the heap by our own strength, we will be frustrated and fearful. Not only that, but our whole idea about success will be twisted.

At one time, I felt great frustrations in terms of my own success as a pastor. I had set out certain goals which I planned to reach, certain attainments which I felt should be mine, and when I was not experiencing them I began to be tormented by that inner hollowness that comes when one feels he is a failure. I shall never forget the release that came to my life, and has stayed with me since, when I finally turned my future over to God. The best I knew how, I exercised trust in that area. I quietly told the Lord that I was willing to stay exactly where I was for the rest of my life if that's where He felt my life could best count. I began to accept where I was, and what I was. Since that time, God has led me in many new paths and blessed me with an inner joy greater than I ever thought possible. I still look back to that time as the moment when I genuinely began to trust God with my future, whatever He chose to make of it.

The truth of the matter is, success is found not in promotions or popularity, but in becoming the kind of person God wants us to be. Once we do that, He will open whatever doors are necessary to allow us to perform the basic task He has for us. But we must exercise trust.

One of the strengths of the apostle Paul is that he learned to have this kind of trust. When he was in jail at Rome, no longer able to preach publicly, no longer able to make missionary journeys, he could easily have become depressed and despairing. But Paul knew the secret of trusting God. He wrote to the Christians at Philippi and affirmed: "The things which happened unto me have fallen out rather unto the furtherance of the gospel" (Phil. 1:12). He went on to explain that because of his imprisonment he had opportunity to share the gospel with the choice bodyguards of Caesar himself. Moreover, his imprisonment had caused many of the other Christians to become more ardent in their own activities to share the good news of the gospel of Christ. On this basis, Paul was assured that everything that was happening was a part of God's divine order. And we know that apart from Paul's imprisonment, many of the letters of the New Testament would never have been written: he wrote them while in chains. The rest of the world has been blessed because his life was circumscribed by a cell.

Pilgrim's Progress would never have been written if John Bunyan, the faithful preacher, had not been imprisoned for years in Bedford jail. The volume for which he is best remembered would never have been penned without his difficult moments. We have no way of knowing what "success" will be in our lives. We have to trust God's wisdom and power to bring it to pass. As Shakespeare observed, "There's a divinity that shapes our ends, rough-hew them how we will."

Or take the example of Joseph, as described in Genesis. As a lad, Joseph was sold into slavery by his jealous brothers. He found himself in faraway Egypt, the slave of another man. Yet the day came when Joseph was second-in-command to Pharaoh himself. After many years, a drought caused Joseph's brothers to come into Egypt searching for food. Joseph was then in a position to provide food for them, and beyond that, to bring them and his father down into Egypt where they could have plenty to eat. The time came when Joseph explained to his brothers why he held no bitterness for them: "As for you, ye thought evil against me; but God meant it unto good, to bring to pass as it is this day, to save much people alive" (Gen. 50:20).

God has the power to take even the evil that is worked against us, and turn it into good. He has the power to bring good out of every circumstance in the lives of those who trust Him (Rom. 8:28). This means that even if our deepest prayers about our personal success are not answered as we desire, God has a different answer because He, better than we, knows what success for us involves.

The words of an anonymous author express this poignantly:

> He prayed for strength that he might achieve;
> He was made weak that he might obey.
> He prayed for health that he might do greater things;
> He was given infirmity that he might do better things.
> He prayed for riches that he might be happy;
> He was given poverty that he might be wise.
> He prayed for power that he might have the praise of men;
> He was given infirmity that he might feel the need of God.
> He prayed for all things that he might enjoy life;
> He was given life that he might enjoy all things.
> He received nothing that he asked for—all that he
>   hoped for;
> His prayer was answered—he was most blessed.[2]

Success, simply stated, is becoming the person God has made it possible for you to be.

Several years ago, *McCall's* carried a lovely story by Marjorie Williams entitled "The Velveteen Rabbit." A velveteen rabbit was given to a little boy one Christmas morning along with many other toys. The mechanical toys seemed to feel especially superior and were quite sure they were real because they had springs and could move. The rabbit, desiring to feel real also, asked the oldest and wisest toy, the skin horse, "What is real? Does it mean having things that buzz inside you and a stick-out handle?"

The horse answered, "Real isn't how you're made, it's a thing that happens to you. When a child loves you for a long, long time, then you become real."

"Does it hurt?" asked the rabbit.

"Sometimes," said the horse, "but when you're real, you don't mind being hurt."

"Does it happen all at once, like being wound up, or bit by bit?"

"It doesn't happen all at once," said the horse. "You become. It takes a long time. That's why it doesn't happen often to people who break easily, or have sharp edges, or who have to be carefully kept. Generally, by the time you are real, most of your hair has been loved off, and your eyes drop out, and you get loose in the joints, and very shabby. But these things don't matter at all, because once you are real, you can't be ugly, except to people who don't understand."

As time passed, the velveteen rabbit was loved by the boy, was left outside in the dew, was dragged around the garden, and did indeed become very shabby. The day came when the nurse tried to throw the bunny away, but the boy cried, "You can't do that. He isn't a toy; he's real." The bunny shivered with joy for he realized that the nursery magic had happened to him. At last he was real!

It is because of God's love that we become real persons. Out of the wholeness thus bestowed on us, we learn to trust our heavenly Father with the method by which He makes us real, and with the circumstances that surround that process.

TRUST GOD WITH YOUR PERSONAL RELATIONSHIPS

Once we have decided to trust God with everything, we can allow that trust to overflow, so that we can begin a healthy trust in all of our human relationships. In other words, we can begin a healthy spirit of trust toward those who are close to us. If your life has been shattered, trust

God to help you build a new life. Then exhibit that trust in an ever-growing way. Go out among people again, trusting God to lead you to new friends. Look for a new job, if the old one has failed, trusting God. I'm not suggesting a naive childishness, but a basic, realistic attitude of trust toward others that operates out of an all-encompassing trust of God.

"Trust me!" says the teen-ager to her mother as she asks for the privilege of going on a weekend trip with a group of other teen-agers, unchaperoned. How do we deal with such situations when they confront us?

First of all, we must realize that trust must be deserved, earned by past performance. We trust God because of His perfect past record of faithfulness. Where our children are concerned, we have to exercise the principle of limited trust in accordance with their ability to face the temptations involved. A boxing manager who cares about his fighter does not match him against just anyone, but rather he carefully selects the opponents lest he prematurely destroy his own man. It is not that the manager does not trust his fighter. But he realizes that trust must be wisely expressed. It is uncaring to place too heavy a burden of trust on someone else, especially on one of our children. They must not be thrust too quickly into new situations for which they are unprepared. There is a foolish "trust" that is not trust at all. But as we trust our children in an ever-enlarging circle, we come at last to the time when they are adults, when they leave the nest, and we can trust them with everything. Until that moment, we allow them to participate in the matter of trust, to earn it gradually. This is the fearsome part of being a parent. One has to gradually turn loose of his child until at last the parent becomes totally unnecessary.

If we are wise, we deal with ourselves the same way. There are some things that we should not pit ourselves against. There are some temptations which each of us should avoid. This is not to distrust oneself, but rather it is trusting one's common sense, one's intuition, one's conscience. As a rule, you will know ahead of time if an event or situation may cause you to betray the trust someone else has placed in you. If so, avoid that situation at all costs.

The matter of trust enters vitally into the marriage relationship. If marriage is to fulfill God's plan, there must be trust involved. What happens when either the husband or the wife betrays the marriage trust? A woman who had discovered her husband had been unfaithful to her once said to me, "How can I ever trust him again?" He had begged her forgiveness and had pledged his future faithfulness. The problem was, could she trust him again? Perhaps the more pointed question is, how would she be able to extend trust to him again?

Since trust between human beings is something which must be earned, we have difficulty understanding how we can trust someone who has betrayed us. However, we must keep in mind that a part of the unfaithful husband's track record was the fact that he had earnestly repented. He recognized that he would have to begin to prove himself trustworthy. The relationship of trust would have to be built up afresh, reconstructed a block at a time. But forgiveness requires us to begin anew a project of trust.

We must keep in mind that all human trust is limited. We have to trust those nearest to us, those who mean something to us, with the awareness of human frailty. This allows us to exhibit human trust without being destroyed if that trust is broken. The wife must either make a decision to extend trust again to her husband, or sever the relationship entirely. It is impossible for a man and his wife to live together in marriage apart from trust.

Some people try to live like the old woman who lived in the shoe. Imagine her having a picnic with her children and trying to hold the hand of each of them every moment. It can't be done. Trust is turning loose so there can be freedom, joy, and individuality. Some of the old woman's children may get in the mud hole, some may climb trees and fall out—but the only way to avoid those things is to cancel the picnic.

The basic decision is simple. You must either relax and trust those who are important to you, or you will smother them with accusations, suspicions, and overprotectiveness. To turn loose is to allow the other person to be himself. Human trust is not based on the perfection of the other person, but on the realization that trust is vital for all relationships. The home is a place where lives are intertwined, but they must never be merged. As Kahlil Gibran wrote:

> Sing and dance together and be joyous,
>   But let each one of you be alone
> Even as the strings of a lute are alone
>   Though they quiver with the same music.
> Stand together yet not too near together
>   For the pillars of the temple stand apart,
> And the oak tree and the cypress
>   Grow not in each other's shadow.[3]

Trust is allowing the other person the right of imperfection, and the right to grow, and the right to develop as a person. There is a sense in which even our trust of God must have something of this dimension. We come to our heavenly Father with our prayers and our requests, and this is well. The Bible indicates that we can come to Him and ask for those things which are on our heart. However, we must always allow God to be free to be Himself—free to be God as He wills, not as we will. Robert Ball observes that even Christ, in His prayers, left the Father free to be the Father. In Gethsemane, Christ shared His innermost feelings with the Father, His agony of soul, but He concluded His prayer by saying, "Nevertheless, not my will but thine be done." He thereby left the way open which allowed God to be God. He made no demands. Perhaps that is one of the highest kinds of prayer that we can offer.[4]

And so we must learn to trust God with all our human relationships. Because we are secure in His hand, we dare to trust others with the knowledge that sometimes they disappoint us. We do so with the knowledge that God's overriding providence will sustain us even when others fail us. When we trust our teen-ager, or our spouse, we are also trusting God to fill in the gap. Every act of trust reaches out beyond the human dimension and lays hold on the promises of God's watch-care. We cannot trust ourselves, or others, in isolation. But our trust is based on a relationship to God.

We cannot grow in human relationships apart from trust. Neither can our loved ones grow and develop apart from our trust in them. We recognize that because God trusts us we have been free to become ourselves. Out of the overflow of His trust extended to us in Jesus Christ, we share that trust in our relationships with others. God has called us His children, given us His name, in trust. There are times when we fail Him, times when we even disgrace Him, but He still calls us His. In those tragic times when human trust has been exhausted, we will trust God to lead us to new relationships where trust can exist. We dare not withdraw all trust, isolate ourselves, or grow a hard shell. If we do that we shall die. We cannot live without trust.

TRUST GOD WITH YOUR HEALTH

Of course, each of us has a responsibility to follow the rules of health. We should strive to rid ourselves of harmful habits. In short, we should do everything we can to be healthy, to use properly the body which God has given us. Beyond that, we need to leave the rest with God, in trust. The alternative is to become a hypochondriac who is convinced that he has every symptom of every disease. We can rest assured that God will either give us good health, or the grace to bear sickness.

To trust God with your health does not mean that you will always be in perfect health. Neither should we suppose that sickness is some punishment for our lack of trust. When illness comes, we need to recognize that God may choose to miraculously heal us, or He may not. In either case, His decision is not based on the level of our faith. Rather, it will be decided according to His divine purposes. Those who promise divine healing to anyone whose faith is sufficient, greatly misread the Scriptures.

The apostle Paul, one of the most faithful men in the Scriptures, lived most of his life with a chronic illness which he referred to as his "thorn in the flesh." We are not told exactly what his illness was, but we do know that at periods it became rather severe. He tells us that on three separate occasions he made a special appeal to

God for divine healing. Yet this man of faith was not healed. God's answer to his prayer was not a miracle, but a promise: "My grace is sufficient for thee: for my strength is made perfect in weakness" (II Cor. 12:9).

Let me share with you my simple definition of grace. Grace is God's offer of Himself. To redeem us from our sins, God offered Himself in Jesus Christ on the cross. In times of trial or illness, God's gift of Himself, His holy presence, enables us to bear whatever pain is ours. The apostle Paul learned that he could trust God with his health. Indeed he found a new depth in his relationship with the Father because of his illness. And so, we hear the apostle say: "Therefore I take pleasure in infirmities, in reproaches, in necessities, in persecutions, in distresses for Christ's sake: for when I am weak, then am I strong" (II Cor. 12:10). We must be careful not to misconstrue what the apostle is saying. He is not happy about his sickness. Rather, he is happy in spite of his sickness, in the midst of his sickness, for he has found Christ to be sufficient.

George Matheson, the noted poet and man of God, lost his sight as a youth and spent forty years in darkness. With God's help he learned to live in that darkness, but more than that, he learned to make use of his handicap. Notice the way he described his own victory:

> My God, I have never thanked thee for my thorn. I have thanked Thee one thousand times for my roses, but never once for my thorn. I have been looking forward to a world where I shall get compensation for my cross, but I never thought of my cross as a present glory. Teach me the glory of my cross. Teach me the value of my thorn. Show me that I have climbed to Thee by the path of pain. Show me that my tears have been my rainbow.[5]

Russell Henry Stafford is right when he says: "Nothing is too good to be true, and nothing bad is final." On the basis of such a promise, we can trust God with our health. When Job's afflictions first began, he kept knocking at heaven's door asking, "Why, why, why?" However, his pilgrimage of pain brought him at last to the place where he realized he was asking the wrong question. He came to recognize that the proper response was to ask, "How?" In other words, we need to ask God how we can best respond to our health, or lack of it. The key to life is our response. Everyone has problems. Everyone has sickness. The important thing is that we ask God how He could have us deal with it. The very center of our response must be trust. God knows what our destiny is. He knows what He would have us accomplish in life. Therefore we can trust Him with the details.

TRUST GOD BEYOND LIFE

As we repeatedly make decisions to trust God in new areas of our life, we shall continually discover that He is trustworthy, and we will therefore be able to come to the time when we can trust Him beyond this life. As we learn to trust Him in the smaller storms, we can trust Him when that final storm besieges us. We must do so with the recognition that faith does not necessarily still the raging winds. Rather, we must trust God in their midst.

On one occasion, Jesus was in a small boat with the disciples on the Sea of Galilee. A sudden storm swept down on the small lake while Jesus was asleep. The disciples excitedly awakened Him saying, "Lord save us: we perish." Jesus' response was a rebuke: "Why are ye fearful, oh ye of little faith?'' (Matt. 8:26). Literally, Jesus called them "little-faiths." They had not yet come to the place where they recognized that His presence with them was enough. They had not yet learned that there is no defeat—not even in death—for those who walk with Christ. Jesus was trying to tell them (and us), "Even if the ship sinks, or the tumor is malignant, or the crash is fatal, you are with Him who holds the universe together, in whose hand is all of life and eternity."[6]

We would do well to learn from the young boy whose father heard him saying, "If you only knew what I know; if you only knew what I know." Curious, the father went into the boy's room to find out what was going on. The answer was simple. The youngster was reading a wild west thriller. He had gotten toward the middle of the book where the plot was thicker and darker with each page and the hero was being abused and disgraced. The gloating villain was winning at every point. At last the youngster could stand it no longer so he turned to the last page of the book to see how the story would turn out. It was there he saw the hero vindicated while the villain was properly punished. Then the youngster went back to the middle of the story where he was able to read it with a peaceful enjoyment. But he could not help saying every now and then, as though he were talking to the villain, "If you only knew what I know."[7]

We rest in the assurance that death itself has been defeated through the resurrection of Jesus Christ. The good news of the gospel is that there is a dimension beyond this present world, an eternity where all things are made new.

Roy Pierson, in discussing the resurrection, observes that Michelangelo would never bomb the Sistine Chapel which contained his frescoes, that Robert Burns would never burn his heartrending songs, that Homer would never throw his *Odyssey* into the sea, that even a poor mountaineer would never destroy the home he had labored years in building. Pierson thus concludes that God would never destroy His best work just when He has begun to use it. This would be like a father leading his children over a long, hard road that leads toward home, affirming his love for them, but planning to kill them all the same before they ever saw the light of home. This, he affirms, would be the picture of God unless He lifts us from the grave.[8]

The certainty of God's providence sheds a new light on birth and death. T. S. Eliot, in "Little Gidding," wrote:

> What we call the beginning is often the end,
> And to make an end is to make a beginning.
> The end is where we start from.

From the Christian stance, life is more than the brief moments between birth and death. Indeed, death is the beginning, the "end we start from." The final chapter belongs to God. The victory is His.[9]

Since the Scripture speaks of heaven as a place where God makes "all things new," we can look on death as God's final healing. In his poem, "The Widow and the Bye Street," John Masefield describes a tragic scene. A little mother, numbed by the anguish of her helplessness and the sense of her failure, watches the execution of her young son who has committed crimes against the state. As the trap door opens and the rope snatches away the son's life, the sobbing mother crumples to the ground and those nearby hear her speak of "broken things, too broke to mend." Life has a way of coming to that. Eventually, circumstances arrive which leave us with "things too broke to mend." At this point death becomes God's touch which heals all our diseases. The resurrection mends all things that have been committed in trust to Jesus Christ.

We really can trust God with everything. He is awake while we sleep. We are blind, but He sees all things. There is no limit to His power. He loves more than we love, cares more than we care. He can salvage good out of everything that happens.

We must make the decision to live in an attitude of trust. The tight-fisted, tensed-up lifestyle is one of the curses of the twentieth century. Trust is an attitude of relaxing your hold on everything, releasing your grip on the future, and beginning to live in the freedom our Lord offers. This means you can resign as general manager of the universe and let God work out the details of the endless maze through which you must pass. Since you cannot by anxious fretting add one day to your life, the more appropriate approach is to live in trust.

Just as we learn to worry, to be anxious, and to live knotted-up lives, so can we learn to turn loose and trust. Let me suggest that you take God at His word on small matters and work your way up. Begin with those things which to you seem to be more tangible. For instance, God promises that those who give one-tenth of their income to His kingdom through the church will be blessed: "Bring ye all the tithes into the storehouse, that there may be meat in mine house, and prove me now herewith, saith the Lord of hosts, if I will not open you the windows of heaven, and pour you out a blessing, that there shall not be room enough to receive it'' (Mal. 3:10). Put this promise to the test. This is something tangible you can do. Keep in mind that God is not promising that you will become rich because you have given one-tenth of your earnings to Him. What He does promise is that a new dimension of blessing will come into your life—blessing from heaven itself. Try this over a period of time. I'm convinced that you will experience a new dimension of life. This will encourage you to place even deeper trust in God.

Or, try going the second mile in one of your personal relationships and see if you do not notice a difference both in yourself and in the other person. If you are worrying about someone over whom you really have no control, try committing him or her in a definite way to the Lord. Make this a real matter of trust. See if you do not have a new sense of peace, even though the danger which concerns you may still exist. Make a list of those things which you have difficulty submitting to God in trust, and determine to take them one at a time, and make the decision to leave them at His throne of grace.

Then, give yourself to life, to living, as one released from chains, and go forward in trust. When King George VI addressed the people of Britain at Christmas time in 1939, the future was dark. The early throes of World War II had engulfed his land. When he came to the microphones of the British Broadcasting System, he used the beautiful words of Minnie Louise Haskins to inspire his people to a new level of faith and trust. I share them now with you, that they may strengthen your heart, attract your focus to Him who stands above the storms, and encourage you to follow in trust God's path of happiness:

And I said to the man who stood at the gate of the year:
"Give me a light, that I may tread safely into the
unknown!"
And he replied: "Go out into the darkness and put your
hand into the Hand of God.
That shall be to you better than light and safer than a
known way."[10]

NOTES

1. Elizabeth O'Connor, *Search for Silence* (Waco, TX: Word Books, 1972), p. 133.

2. In "Prayer Poems," compiled by O. V. and Helen Armstrong (Nashville: Abingdon-Cokesbury Press, 1942), p. 219.

3. Kahlil Gibran, *The Prophet* (New York: Alfred A. Knopf, 1951), pp. 15–16.

4. Robert R. Ball, *The "I Feel" Formula* (Waco, TX: Word Books, 1977), pp. 93–94.

5. *Christianity Today* (November 8, 1963), p. 54.

6. B. W. Woods, *Understanding Suffering* (Grand Rapids: Baker Book House, 1974), p. 142.

7. *Pulpit Digest* (January-February, 1977), p. 31.

8. Roy Pierson, *The Believer's Unbelief* (New York: Thomas Nelson and Sons, 1963) p. 156, quoting Arthur Wentwood Hewitt, *Jerusalem the Golden*, pp. 105–107.

9. Helmut Thielicke, *I Believe* (Philadelphia: Fortress Press, 1968), p. 202ff.

10. Ralph Murray, *From the Beginning* (Nashville: Broadman Press, 1964), p. 129, quoting Minnie Louise Haskins, "The Gate of the Year," *Masterpieces of Religious Verse,* p. 92.